Conquering Digital Overload

Peter Thomson · Mike Johnson
J. Michael Devlin
Editors

Conquering Digital Overload

Leadership Strategies that Build
Engaging Work Cultures

A FutureWork Forum publication

Editors
Peter Thomson
FutureWork Forum
Henley-on-Thames, UK

J. Michael Devlin
FutureWork Forum
Brussels, Belgium

Mike Johnson
FutureWork Forum
Lymington, Hampshire, UK

ISBN 978-3-319-63798-3   ISBN 978-3-319-63799-0   (eBook)
https://doi.org/10.1007/978-3-319-63799-0

Library of Congress Control Number: 2017951549

Cover design by Samantha Johnson

Printed on acid-free paper

This Palgrave Macmillan imprint is published by Springer Nature
The registered company is Springer International Publishing AG
The registered company address is: Gewerbestrasse 11, 6330 Cham, Switzerland

In memory of Richard Smith, whose untimely death during the writing of this book was a great loss to the FutureWork Forum

Preface

It was the American actor W.C. Fields who allegedly coined the phrase, 'never work with children or animals', something that has remained a sobering, all too often, truism to this day. And, of course, it depends on your gullibility, or let's just say the attraction of the new fad of *fake news*, as whether or not you believed whether he actually said that (he was rumoured, like the film-maker Sam Goldwyn, to employ an army of gag writers).

Whatever the truth, there is another truism we may want to take on board, depending on how logical, gripping, educational, entertaining or informative that you find the next hundred or so pages, that you should never, ever agree to co-write anything. I've been a solo writer for my whole life (authored 50+ books, thousands of articles studies and research papers, without resorting to a co-writer). So why, at an age when my 70th birthday beckons, should I break the rule that has kept me gainfully employed since I first wrote for my local newspaper at the tender age of 16?

To compound the felony, if you look at the cover, you'll see we have erred thrice, and opted for not one but three co-authors.

Worse still take a look at the contents pages at the front, and you'll see we have included others, Belgians, Dutch, Finns, Germans, Swiss, even the odd Brit feeling the breeze of Brexit on their creative, furrowed brows, aided by the Americans still woozy from Trump's Tweets adding to the digital din.

Yes, we have committed the ultimate publishing sin and produced a book that involves the many. All our efforts in pursuit of that elusive phrase. The all too difficult to define—the 'Digital Age'.

Like all good ideas, it started with a meeting of the FutureWork Forum. A group of 30 or so professionals who come together several times each year to discuss the emerging issues of the world of work and the workplace and how we as individuals or organizations fit into it. For the past 20 or so years, we've produced some good studies, hosted a score of conferences and offered our opinions to corporations, international organizations and governments.

This time we went a stage further and opted to 'do' a book—pooling the collective wisdom of the FutureWork Forum partners (the title we have grandly bestowed upon ourselves). At first, it was a bit of fun. It was our Austrian/American partner, Peter Vogel, whose work and worries about the increasing digital pressure in our organizations first came to our attention. From that early start, the enthusiasm of our publisher, Stephen Partridge, drove us forward and we soon had our ringmaster in place. Peter Thomson became the de facto whip-cracker-in-chief, chivvying us ever onward, cheered from the sidelines by everyone who added to the mix. Michael Devlin, Peter Thomson and I had a mad 2-day editorial scramble in Brussels to pull together strands from the Partners. This was followed by another meeting in London where we were joined by Richard Savage, Michael Staunton and Andrew Chadwick. Richard and Michael have followed up energetically to put the final manuscript to bed.

And the result? Should we have done it? Well it's not perfect, but it does achieve one great thing. It shows what a lot of trouble we are in. This Digital Age ain't that fun to be in. Yes, we would have liked to solve the problem of digital overload (provide the silver bullet), but we missed by a mile.

However, we are very proud of one thing. We took on a task that seemed crazy and we made it. We haven't found all the answers, but we have stated the case, we know where the booby traps in your business are, even if we can't seize the smoking gun. There is so much value in this book, but it needs to be read with your eyes open (and preferably your phone and email switched off). If you read it, it will reward you with an insight into the huge challenges facing the workplace and the world of work today. Read properly, it should point you to some answers. More importantly, it should act as a guide as to what to do next.

What it has proved beyond all doubt is that the power of collaboration is alive and well and the power of our FutureWork Forum colleagues' collective thoughts and actions has prevailed. And there wasn't an animal or a child in sight, either!!

I'd like to thank for their huge enthusiasm, Peter Vogel, Göran Hultin, Richard Savage, Michael Staunton, Alain Haut, Ben Emmens, Cliff Dennett Jim Ware, Susan Stucky, Matthiass Mölleney, Sunnie Groeneveld, Andrew Chadwick, Larissa Hämisegger, Michael Devlin and Peter Thomson.

I hope it makes you think, makes you act and helps you free yourself of the bits, bytes and chains from the digital slavery we have brought upon ourselves.

Thanks again to Peter Thomson and Richard Savage, two great editors, with a true sense of style.

Lymington, Hampshire   Mike Johnson
October 2017

Acknowledgements

The editors are grateful to all the partners of the FutureWork Forum who have contributed to this publication. This has been a team effort. Names of authors appear against each chapter, but many of them have contributed to other sections of the book.

We are also grateful to Stephen Partridge of Palgrave Macmillan who helped us to develop the initial idea and supported us through the process of pulling together the strands into a coherent whole.

Contents

Editors and Contributors

About the Editors

Peter Thomson is an expert on the future of work and co-author of the best-selling book 'Future Work'. He is a director of Wisework Ltd and advises senior managers on adapting organization cultures to new ways of working. After a career in HR in the IT sector, he set up the Future Work Forum at Henley Business School and ran it for 16 years. He is a regular speaker at conferences on topics relating to the future of work and leadership. He is now a Director of FutureWork Forum Ltd and is responsible for the operations of this international association of consultants.

Mike Johnson is chairman and founder of the FutureWork Forum. He is a leading commentator, consultant and writer on the Future of Work, Talent Management, Corporate Communications and How to Work as an Independent. He is the author of 12 books on business and management issues and a regular presenter on conferences around the globe. He has written several series of world-of-work studies for both The Economist and the Financial Times, as well as over 100 global and Europe-wide studies for international corporations and institutions. He has developed a long-standing reputation as a researcher and reporter on a wide range of organizational issues.

J. Michael Devlin is a science and policy communication professional. For the past 15 years, he has led and managed teams for international research centres and consortia in the areas of agriculture, health research systems, forestry, environmental management and rural development. He is a co-founder of Sci4D—The Science for Development Platform—a new service that makes public research and programme results more accessible to decision-makers and investors, and offers synthesis and capacity building services. This initiative aims to make all 'public goods' research available in a standard format—to open this hidden knowledge to the world.

Contributors

Andrew Chadwick is a London-based architect and a global pioneer of the use of CAD in architecture. He invented the Organizational SpaceTime Modelling technique for the establishment and manipulation of space requirements. He applied his SpaceTime approach to a pilot scheme for the then Andersen Consulting in London, arguably the world's first working virtual office. As a result, he moved Accenture into the most prestigious building on the Champs Elysees in Paris creating the first truly working non-territorial office in the world. Latterly, he designed a 1000-person office in India without aircon using passive design principles. He believes the combination of SpaceTime and Passive Design is the way forward for our world's built environment.

Cliff Dennett is Head of Business Development for Innovation Birmingham, the UK's largest campus dedicated to digital entrepreneurs and SMEs. He therefore spends his time mentoring many digital start-up and growth business leadership teams. He specializes in building new revenue streams 'from the ground up'. Previously, as founding CEO of start-up, Soshi Games, Cliff spent over 5 years building a digital music-games business, raising £1.4 m investment and completing deals with some of the biggest rock bands on the planet. He has extensive experience in corporates and SMEs, having worked in sales, strategy and operations for companies including Orange, Hewlett Packard and AT&T. Cliff has spoken around the world on innovation and entrepreneurship.

Ben Emmens is a senior consultant with more than 15 years international experience in leadership, management and consulting. He has particular expertise in Human Resources Management and Organization Development in the non-profit sector where he has consulted, taught and written on organizational strategy, governance, leadership development, capacity assessment and development and a wide range of people management issues. He has worked in more than 40 countries around the world, for well-known non-profits such as UNICEF, Save the Children, Oxfam, Action Aid, the Scouts and the International Rescue Committee. His book 'Conscious Collaboration' was published by Palgrave Macmillan in 2016.

Sunnie Groeneveld is a Managing Partner of Inspire 925, a consulting firm that helps companies increase employee engagement, collaboration and innovation through digital solutions. She also co-founded Lunch-Lottery.com and has been selected by the leading Swiss business newspaper Handelszeitung for their 'Top 50 Who is Who in Digital Switzerland'. She wrote the book 'Inspired at Work' in 2014 and is a regular contributor to HR Today and The Huffington Post. She holds an Economics degree from Yale University and is a member of the European Digital Leaders Network established by the World Economic Forum.

Larissa Hämisegger followed her business studies with work as an organizational developer in different start-ups and small businesses, developing the business, the organizational culture and the employer brand by working on strategy, processes and people development. She then founded UNUMONDO, a language coaching and integration service, where internationals learn the local language applied in real life with a local instead of in the classroom with books. She is fluent in five languages herself and understands a couple more. Larissa is also a yoga and meditation instructor and introduces such practices into workspaces as she sees great importance in bridging personal wellbeing, mindfulness and business.

Alain Haut enjoyed a 35-year corporate career in a global role with leading multinational companies (in automotive, high technology and life sciences) mainly in International Human Resources Management. In 2008, Alain established O plc, a management consulting company specializing in the fields of Performance, Leadership (development and acquisition) and Change, as well as Human Resources matters in general (including coaching). In addition to consulting activities, Alain is a regular lecturer on Leadership, Talent Management and Human Resources at several business schools in Switzerland, France and Ukraine at Doctorate, Master and Bachelor levels. Alain is Corporate Peer Reviewer for EQUIS and EPAS business schools and programmes accreditation and corporate member of the EPAS Accreditation Board with EFMD.

Göran Hultin combines international and national experience of labour markets with private sector industry and business experience. He has more than 15 years of experience in international labour market legislation and regulation. Recently, he was Assistant Director General of the ILO and Executive Director of the Employment Sector. He now works with governments and leading organizations on policy and practice by building public private partnerships to improve labour performance and business strategy, aligning business goals with corporate values, building management—labour relations, developing training strategies to meet skill and competency needs.

Matthias Mölleney is a leadership and change management expert with more than 15 years of experience in senior executive positions. He is the founder of the HR consulting, coaching and training company peopleXpert. He also leads the Centre for Human Resources Management and Leadership at the University for Applied Sciences in Economics Zurich (HWZ) and is the President of the largest professional Human Resources Management Association in Switzerland (ZGP). In 1998, he became Executive Vice President Human Resources Management and member of the executive board at Swissair. He is a well-known speaker, lecturer and author with a great deal of practical experience in leadership and change management.

Richard Savage has held senior international HR leadership roles in Cadbury Schweppes, Quaker Oats and Nielsen, where he led major successful change initiatives and ensured the HR function added real business value. He now consults, acts a coach and mentor across a wide range of companies, industries and individuals. He is a firm believer in engagement, inclusive talent and leadership development and of the need for a new model of leadership to meet today's societal challenges. His passion for helping individuals extends to his pro-bono support and is matched by his passion for his family and Arsenal football club.

Michael Staunton is an experienced talent/learning professional and coach focused on driving change and transformation working with individuals, teams and organizations. As an international leader, he has developed broad experience in organizational development as well as driving leadership and building effective talent management strategies and approaches. Michael has run talent and transformation programmes in telecoms, services, brewing, engineering, hi-tech and finance sectors. Michael was formerly Programme Director for Management Centre Europe based in Brussels, Global Vice President Organization and Development and Learning with Interbrew (now Anheuser Busch) in Leuven Belgium, and Head of Talent Development EMEA for State Street Bank in London. Michael was awarded a Doctorate in Business Administration through Portsmouth University in 2014.

Susan Stucky Since leaving IBM Research in 2014, Susan has been working as an advisor and consultant to institutes such as mediaX at Stanford, as part of thought leadership teams such as the Collabworks' TLT, and with established companies and Silicon Valley start-ups alike. The consulting approaches she brings are scale agnostic—they play well in large ecosystems and small start-ups. Presently, her areas of focus include the design of work marketplaces and of service systems for value co-creation. As always, this work includes collaborating with clients to design and develop new ways of working in the face of new technology, new business process or facilities.

Peter Vogel is Professor of Family Business and Entrepreneurship at IMD in Lausanne, a serial technology entrepreneur, business advisor and speaker. He's founder and chairman of the Delta Venture Partners

AG. He previously served as director of custom programmes at the Executive School of the University of St.Gallen and as chairman of the HR Matching AG. In his work with companies, he focuses on topics such as global megatrends and their impact on organizations, growth and internationalization, digital transformation, innovation management and intrapreneurship, as well as leadership and talent development. He's a frequent speaker at global conferences such as the Global Economic Symposium, TEDxLausanne or the St.Gallen Symposium, author of books and book chapters and a member of the Global Shapers Community of the World Economic Forum.

Jim Ware is a professional speaker, a workplace futurist, and a meeting design strategist. A former Harvard Business School professor, he has invested his entire career in understanding what organizations must do to thrive in a rapidly changing world—and enabling them to succeed. He is the founder and executive director of The Future of Work … unlimited, a research and advisory firm based in northern California. He has co-authored several books and research reports about the digital economy and its implications for leadership and organizational performance. His most recent book is 'Making Meetings Matter: How Smart Leaders Orchestrate Powerful Conversations in the Digital Age'.

1

Introduction: Digitalization and Why Leaders Need to Take It Seriously

Peter Vogel and Göran Hultin

We are living in an era of unprecedented change and transformation. Never before have we and our cumulative knowledge evolved in such a rate as what we can observe today. Today's leaders need to proactively respond to many challenges that result from the 'new normal' we live in; that is the VUCA world—a world that is volatile, uncertain, complex and ambiguous. Among various drivers of this VUCA world is digital technology. As Klaus Schwab, founder of the World Economic Forum put it: 'In the new world, it is not the big fish which eats the small fish, it's the fast which which eats the slow fish'.[1] Digitalization has brought forth new players that attack the behemoths of the twentieth century, with novel business models and an agile market entry strategy. Hence, organizations

P. Vogel (✉)
FutureWork Forum, Zurich, Switzerland
e-mail: vogelpm@gmail.com

G. Hultin
FutureWork Forum, Geneva, Switzerland
e-mail: g.hultin@cadenglobal.com

© The Author(s) 2018
P. Thomson et al. (eds.), *Conquering Digital Overload*,
https://doi.org/10.1007/978-3-319-63799-0_1

1

need to be agile and respond to these disruptive forces if they want to maintain and consolidate their position in the global economy.

Digitalization presents businesses with unparalleled opportunities for value creation. New products and services can be offered and commercialized, systems and processes can be optimized, work processes can be automated and digital business models can be developed. All-in-all, one can say that those companies have have done particularly well over the past decades in adopting digital technologies in their everyday business—possibly even cannibalizing their own business in the process, with novel digitalized offerings—have not only survived this transformation, but also done disproportionately well, financially. In a recent study, MIT and CapGemini showed that the so-called digirati firms—firms that are strong in both the digital intensity and transformation intensity systematically outperform other companies in terms of revenues, profitability and market valuation.[2] In the world of work, digitalization has opened up many new avenues for organizations and their employees, such as facilitated communication and collaboration between employees around the world, improved recruiting, talent management processes and workplace flexibility that allows organizations to adjust to their employees' personal situations, as well as better performance management.

Despite all these undisputable flexible advantages of digitalization, it also brings with it a variety of problems for organizations and individuals. On an individual level, we are confronted with an information overload and constant distraction from our core activities. Indeed, what has become self-evident is that the information accessible on the internet is literally exploding. At the same time, our consumption of material on the internet is at an incredibly high level, with roughly a mind-numbing 2.5 million Google search queries, 2.8 million YouTube video views, 21 million WhatsApp messages and 700,000 Facebook logins happening every minute[3].

On an organizational level, issues such as cyber security, the cost of keeping on top of the evolution of digital technology or digital distraction and overload of employees are some of many downside effects of the digital age we now occupy. Moore's law—that the computing power of processors doubles every 18 months—and Nielsen's law—that bandwidth doubles approximately every 21 months—clearly underscore the rate of change. This implies that novel technological solutions are available every couple of months, requiring organizations to invest great amounts of time and money to (1) stay up-to-date and (2) make sure that all their employees are sufficiently trained in using the new systems effectively and efficiently. As a byproduct of all this, employees are increasingly losing control over their own time, because digital systems such as emails, internal chatrooms, etc., are taking over their agenda in that they constantly need to react and respond to incoming information (some important, some irrelevant) instead of proactively managing their time.

The following fictitious case illustrates an exemplary day of a family in the digital era:

A 21st Century day in the lives of Johan and Jeanette:

Meet Johan, a 42-year-old Senior Manager at a large company and his 41-year-old wife Jeanette, a Marketing Manager at a communication consulting firm. Johan and Jeanette have two children, 17 and 14 years old. Johann has a 30-minute commute to work and despite having a 40-hour work week, he spends on average 50 hours at work, plus several hours from home. Jeanette works 80% on paper, but actually spends a lot more time on work-related matters than that.

Johan's day starts by waking up at 6am from his smartphone's alarm clock. The first thing Johan does after waking up is to quickly check the number of emails that came in since he last checked his mail the past evening. He'll scroll through them and delete spam and other non-relevant mails. After taking a shower and getting dressed, Johan sits at the breakfast table with his family. This is the time to check the news and what has happened in the world. While he used to read the newspaper, he now follows the news on his tablet, like most other smart mobile device owners. Jeanette needs to check the news first thing in the morning in order to stay up-to-date on her clients' latest news coverage. Their children also have their phones on the table, checking news, emails, Facebook, WhatsApp and Snapchat updates.

At 7.30am, everyone leaves the house to drive to work or go to school. A quick goodbye, of course with the mobile phone in their hands. Johann commutes to work by car, Jill takes the public transportation. During the commute, Johan thinks about his day and what he wants to get done. In order to keep track of it, he dictates these tasks to his phone using voice control, or else he will forget about everything once arriving at work. Jeanette continues working through her mails and client-related news in order to get ready for work.

Once they have arrived at work, both immediately sit down and try to get to work with a clear task list and agenda of meetings for the day. They spend their day in front of the screen—both at their desk and in meetings when taking notes. As always, their agenda is being disrupted by incoming messages via mail, social media and other channels, eating up about half of their productive work time.

At 6 pm, they make their way home again. A quick conversation with their kids about their days, followed by dinner—again with mobile phones at the table—and some family time, before everybody retrieves to whatever they have to get done before going to bed. Kids chat with their friends in a variety of different messaging systems. Johan and Jeanette take a quick last glimpse at the email inbox and a final scroll down the Facebook and news updates, before their phones are put to flight mode and the lights are turned off. 'Good night, Johan'. 'Good night Jeanette'.

Footnote: Johan and Jeanette are just fictitious characters, but the situation described above most likely resonates—at least in part—with most of us. We feel overwhelmed, constantly stressed and upset because we never seem to get the things done we intended to.

The drivers for this digital overload are manifold, including both personal and workplace-related drivers. As illustrated above, we ourselves are largely responsible for this, simply because we haven't yet adjusted our behavior to digitalization and we are just starting to understand the entire spectrum of downside effects resulting from the 'always-connected lifestyle' most of us follow. We lack the necessary discipline to set ourselves boundaries when it comes to utilizing digital technology at home and at work. Simultaneously, we aren't sufficiently aware of the degree to which digital technology is invading our privacy.

At work, it is to some extent also a lack of discipline, but at the same time it is a consequence of an already outdated leadership style and the subsequent false management expectations they create. Setting rules of collaboration and communication in the digital context is one of many necessary steps that leaders need to take in order to avoid digital overload in the workplace. With Digital Natives—individuals born at or after the introduction of the internet—entering the workforce, it is becoming even more important that organizations think about strategies to handle digital overload of their employees. Why? Because Digital Natives are even more exposed to digital technologies than previous generations and have a tendency to spend significantly more time on various social platforms than their older peers.

The consequences from an 'always-connected lifestyle' for ourselves and for organizations are manifold. Most of us live in an always-connected mode, where personal and professional life are hardly separated by any useful 'firewalls', preventing us from taking time off to reboot our system. It is shown that there are many health-related issues resulting from digitalization (in the broadest sense), starting with back and posture problems from sitting in front of and staring at screens, neck problems from staring into mobile phones, as well as a variety of psychological issues such as digital depression, digital burnout, amongst others. Levels of stress are rising because we seem to never get done with our work. At the same time, our interpersonal relations are being disrupted, (just ask Johan and Jeanette about their sex lives!) with more and more of it happening in virtual environments. Yet, with all its positives and opportunities for the future, technology continues to bring about challenges.

Organizations have started to realize that digital overload of their employees has major downside effects on the overall organizational performance. Disengaged employees (for example because of digital burnout) cost organizations across the globe hundreds of billions of dollars each year (Gallup).[4] In Germany, sick days related to psychological illness increased by 70% from 2010 to 2013.[5] The estimated cost to business was €8-10 billion.[6] According to a study conducted in the UK, one in three HR Directors said 'employee burnout' was common in their organization, mainly because of workload and long hours.[7] Eighty percent of managers are concerned that it leads to them losing their key talent. Moreover, work related stress is not only a Western problem. The severity of burnout, even suicides due to workload, is well documented in countries like China, Japan and South Korea. In

Japan, for instance, according to the International Labour Office, in the 14 years between 1997 and 2011, the number of compensated cases of work related death or suicides increased from 49 to 187.[8] The causality between technology and work-related stress may be unclear but the concurrence of increased technology at the workplace and work related stress symptoms is compelling.

Besides the individual and the organizational level, there are societal and labor market consequences of digital transformation. Labor markets and legislations are still deeply rooted in the 'old economy', with metrics assuming standard employment relationships, regular working hours and a physical workplace, ignoring modern forms of work that are enabled as a result of digital technology. A timely example for the 'unreadiness' of politics for the digital disruption of the world of work is the ongoing regulatory resistance against Uber as it applies technology to open up and improve access to taxi services for providers as well as customers. Moreover, regulation does not specifically deal with technology induced stress or psychological symptoms.

It is a worrisome truth that, today most organizations use twenty first century technology, but with an operational twentieth century mindset, processes and organizational structures. Today's leaders, both in businesses and in politics, need to assume their responsibilities and put in place structures and systems to create a workplace of the future; one where the employees' engagement and well-being is at least equally important as organizational efficiency and performance. The good news is that many major firms have started to think about digital transformation; the bad news, however, is that most still lack an overall, holistic approach. This represents a great opportunity, because while we have been reacting to technological innovation, constantly chasing the newest trends and gadgets, we can now finally start to set rules for human behaviour when it comes to how and when to use digital technology. When is it useful and when not? Employers and managers now have a golden opportunity to define a clear digital strategy that will help their organization succeed in the mid to long term.

Overview of Book

This book discusses the challenges resulting from digital overload and what leaders need to watch out for in order to avoid burning out their people. It contains tips for leaders that they can implement now. In the final chapter we point to the future but the introduction is about the problems we have now and the fact that leaders need to act today if they want to maintain a talented workforce.

Here is a summary of what we cover in each chapter.

The first two chapters look at the **symptoms** that are telling us there is a serious problem with Digital Overload. In Chap. 2, we take a close look at the people issues. All too often in a machine-led world, the people are the last things we think about. This chapter sets out to address how we get people back to the center of the engagement equation.

Chapter 3 explains why this Digital Age is a business issue. Most importantly it asks why leaders have done such a lousy job keeping people on their agendas

The next two chapters focus on the **causes** of Digital Overload. Chap. 4 examines what impact having, or NOT having an effective corporate culture has on how well you navigate the digital rapids that flow through all our organizations

Chapter 5 lays out the technology issues and why we are still struggling with it.

We then move on to **solutions** starting with Chap. 6 that points a spotlight on the experiences of us humans in the workplace and our struggle to make sense of the digital world around us.

Into Chap. 7, it's all about how to build a more effective workplace and the rules for doing that and this flows directly into Chap. 8 where we discuss creating a viable, engaging environment that people want to be and work in.

Chapter 9 asks what governments, companies, and individuals can do to mitigate and possibly leverage Digital Overload

Chapter 10 is focused on developing effective coping strategies to deal successfully with the digital age, which leads us directly onto Chap. 11

where we discuss how technology can provide the solution se are all seeking.

Finally we move from today's solutions to look further into the **future**. In Chap. 12 we close down with the provocative thought about whether we are going to see what many have called 'the death of work'.

2

How Employees Are Impacted

Richard Savage and Michael Staunton

The 24/7 world of work is having a significant impact on employees with disastrous consequences for individuals and the organizations that employ them. This chapter explores each of the aspects that are often dehumanizing work and storing up problems that need to be addressed, yet mostly ignored—the curse that is email overload; the rise of stress and depression among employees; the impact of the lack of engagement on employees and the organization; the rise and impact of 'gig' workers and the myth that is multi-tasking. Leaders need to recognize the impact that digital overload is having on their employees. The world of work has changed dramatically over the past decade yet leadership models are lagging these changes with significant adverse impact on employees.

R. Savage (✉)
FutureWork Forum, London, UK
e-mail: rs@futureworkforum.com

M. Staunton
FutureWork Forum, Winchester, UK
e-mail: michaelstaunton@mac.com

© The Author(s) 2018
P. Thomson et al. (eds.), *Conquering Digital Overload*,
https://doi.org/10.1007/978-3-319-63799-0_2

Introduction

Practically every article you read on the 'digital economy', or 'the Fourth Industrial Revolution', as it's been called, suggests it can solve all your issues. Whether it be increasing your ability to understand and reach your target audience, delight your customers, speed up your supply chain and any and all your projects, the 'solution' it would seem is digital. The 'outcome' will be increased productivity and profitability.

Congratulations if that accurately describes your organization. For the vast majority though, it clearly isn't happening. Business investment is falling and productivity has plateaued across the developed world. It is one of the biggest issues we are facing. For years before digital, productivity rose, mainly as a result of investment. That allowed organizations to give their employees pay rises and that helped raise standards of living. Without productivity rises, employees can't look forward to pay increases and are condemned to lower standards of living than their parents enjoy.

So, the nirvana promised by doing things digital hasn't happened yet. Its pervasiveness is already very clear and will only increase with the Internet of Things and Artificial Intelligence still to fully develop. When the label 'the Fourth Industrial Revolution' was given to this, most people thought that while jobs would be lost, new better ones would be created, as has happened before.

What Have We Got Out of This?

What has this Fourth Industrial Revolution brought us so far? Well, the revolution hasn't started yet. At this time, we are about one year away from a similar period in history; where France was before the French Revolution of the Eighteenth Century. Think about it. The impact so far has been that all the benefits have gone to a few digital billionaires/multi-millionaires who have done little or nothing for society in general, maybe even negative benefits for society if their companies aren't paying their fair share of taxes. It's much like the French nobility who garnered all the wealth while doing nothing but look after themselves and watch the peasants starve. While 'starving' may not be commonplace today, certainly it's not so different to the vast majority who find themselves locked into ever increasing work demands from their masters and an overload of tasks for, at best, the same pay as they received before the 'revolution'. While the proletariat may not revolt in the same way as did the French, there is clearly a huge swell of disillusionment rising. Wealth inequality continues to worsen. The backlash against egregious CEO salary levels is an example, with more publicity, shareholders and fund managers revolting. 'Zero hours' contracts, is another example, where there are no guarantees of how many hours per week employees might get to work. This may suit some people, but for many the inability to know whether they will get 10 or 40 hours work, week to week, puts huge pressure on them.

It's Always Been Like This

There are those who suggest that 'it's always been like this', it is nothing new. There have always been high demands on employees, a culture of the need to work long hours and authoritarian leaders who were indifferent to the needs of employees. It was situations like this that gave birth to the 'work-life balance' movement that arose in the 70s and 80s. Employees, and some forward thinking organizations, felt the conflict between work and family demands to be skewed in favour of the working population and this led to tensions and dissatisfaction.

But now, we're in a different time. The boundary between work and life is significantly more blurred than ever as we are now more accessible than ever. The smartphone on its own has ensured that and, in general, organizations have encouraged this. You don't need to be visible to your boss. He/she is quite relaxed if you work from home for a day, or in a coffee shop (well possibly that depends on what kind of boss you have, for many, presenteeism is still all the rage). The invisible cord that links you to your boss at all times is the technology of the smartphone. Previously, when you left the office, you were out of reach. And, while it may suit many to have the 'freedom' of working remotely, the lack of social interaction isn't conducive to collaboration and a shared vision. Today, the expectation is that your smartphone is constantly by your side and that you will check work issues in between checking your Twitter/Snapchat/Facebook feed. That's another aspect that makes this time very different to before, the sheer amount of potential distractions to vie for your attention.

We Are Drowning

One other aspect the digital world has brought us is this vast amount of information we are both creating and being exposed to. Even ten years ago, the University of Southern California published a study[9] that showed the amount of information each of us produces each day had risen nearly two hundred fold between 1986 and 2007 as we moved from word processors that only a few employees had access to, faxes and 'snail mail' to email and social networks—and 2007 was before we started using Twitter and Facebook. The sheer deluge of information we are now subjected to is a distraction from achieving many of the things that really matter.

Also, while difficult to quantify, can anybody doubt that the speed of change in organizations is exponentially faster than twenty years ago? How many reorganizations are there? How many changes in design, demands to get new products to market more quickly, how many more alliances between companies? Another aspect is the rise of 'gig workers'. An EY (Ernst & Young) survey[10] in the USA in June 2016, 'The gig economy is transforming the workforce', suggests that 'gig workers', also known as 'contingent workers' will continue to become a larger proportion of the workforce. While some may feel this a positive change, others, who prefer the certainty of employment, will find this way of life more precarious with a consequent impact on their performance.

The issues that are affecting your employees, and having a huge negative impact on their motivation and their effectiveness, are covered below. None of these should be a surprise. But the reality is that leaders aren't responding to the genuine needs of their employees, nor organizing their employees' working environments to counter these.

The 'Digital' Curse that Is Email

Email is the symptom of the issues that digital technology has brought us. Surely, when we first started using it, we thought there would be benefits; the ability to communicate more quickly, instantly to a wide audience, freeing up time spent trying to contact others, enabling better and faster decision-making. Or, put another way, increasing productivity. Sadly, it has turned into a tyranny that exacerbates the 24/7 culture that is permeating organizations, driven by the ability to check and work on emails by smartphone.

So far, those who keep predicting the death of email have been proved wrong. There's plenty of evidence to show that the number of email accounts and the number of emails we send and receive daily are continuing to increase. The Radicati Group, a California based technology market research organization, in their 'Email Statistics Report'[11] estimate that the number of business emails sent and received per user per day was 124 in 2016 and it is continuing to increase. And by 2020, they estimate that nearly half the world's population will be using email. So if you hoped it was dying out, sorry to disillusion you! To give you an idea of the extent to which this is a concern, a McKinsey study[12] in 2012 showed that interaction workers spent an average of 28% of their time answering emails and another 20% looking for internal information. That is one huge diversion of potentially productive time!

To Turn Off, or, How to Turn Employees off?

In an attempt to address the impact of 24/7 email, a number of companies, such as VW, have taken actions like turning off the server after 5.00 pm or stopping staff receiving emails while on holiday. All these and similar actions may appear positive, at least in terms of looking after employees' wellbeing. There's two big 'buts' though.

Surely one of the advantages of connectability is that we can work remotely, from home or from a coffee shop or use the train commute to some benefit. If we need to take a couple of hours for a child or parent care, or take an emergency trip to a dentist, surely we should be happy to take some time in the evening to catch up? It's all part of an adult environment where there is give and take on both sides. It seems retrograde to go back to an era where we 'clock on and clock off'. A wet Sunday afternoon if the spouse has taken the children visiting, may be just the time to settle down. This 'adult' approach was given further credibility by the UK's Chartered Institute of Personnel and Development (CIPD), Spring 2017 'Employee Outlook' survey.[13] 52% of those surveyed said that remote access to the workplace 'helped them to work flexibly', and only 10% disagreed, and 42% said it 'helped them to stay in control of their workload'. However, almost a third of employees (32%) agreed that remote access to the workplace means they can't switch off in their personal time. Almost a fifth (18%) said it makes them feel as though they are under surveillance, with 17% saying remote access to the workplace makes them anxious and impacts their sleep quality.

The other big 'but' is, if we frown or restrict working on emails outside of working hours, then all emails will have to be dealt with during the working day. Think about that in terms of your organization's productivity. Coming back from a week's vacation would be a nightmare and the first two days back will be a blur as we try to work through the mountain of mails. There's also the worrying feeling of satisfaction from getting to the end of a string of unopened emails, even though this achievement has done little to advance the tasks that actually need performing.

Recently, France has passed a law that gives employees the 'right to disconnect' from emails once their normal day has ended. This approach also finds favor with UK employees. From the same CIPD survey,[14] 2017 'Employee Outlook', 77% of those questioned said employees 'should have the right to disconnect from technology' and only 5% disagreed. However, the leader of the organization always sets the expectation. In one interview conducted for this book, an employee of a global services company said 'I know, in theory, I don't have to answer emails, but my boss and many others in this organization are hell-bent on their own, individual success and feel that driving us harder is their right as it may improve the way they are viewed. I have a great marriage and two kids and I fear that putting them first will affect my chances'.

Restricting when I can work is simply exacerbating the problem that needs addressing at source. The loss of productivity and the personal time invasion caused by email overload and the expectation of 24/7 accessibility has to be high on every leader's agenda when assessing their ideal company culture.

There are alternatives to email that are gaining credibility, like Slack, Hipchat, Jive, Yammer, etc. These are not a panacea. There are plenty who will say they are just another form of digital tyranny. What they can provide is a searchable base of information that email doesn't. It's relatively easy for a new start-up to avoid the pitfalls of email. Not so easy when email has been deep into the fabric of your organization for many years and, as we've seen earlier, the number of business emails sent per day continues to rise inexorably!

Here's the example of the Halton Housing Trust, as reported in the UK's The Times in June 2016[15]; 'Now a housing trust in Cheshire has picked up the baton and is preparing to turn off its internal server after a two-year programme to wean staff off emails. The Halton Housing Trust worked out that staff were spending 40% of their time on internal emails.

Nick Atkin, the chief executive, said he feared that his employees were 'addicted' so only drastic action would work. The trust started off naming and shaming its highest email users in a monthly league table, while developing its intranet for more sophisticated internal communications.

An email charter limits the use of functions such as 'reply to all' and 'cc'. It encourages staff to check external emails only once or twice a day, with an auto-response warning clients not to expect prompt replies. The Trust was coming close to its goal of turning off its internal server. Mr Atkin said. 'What is clear is that email has become an overused and abused communication tool. Instead of being one of many ways to hold conversations it has become the default tool,' he said.'

Don't Underestimate the Impact of Stress and Depression

The macho culture where leaders set the tone of 24/7 accessibility is causing huge damage to both the health of individuals and thus to organizations. The latest statistics are hugely worrying. The World Health Organization[16] (WHO) having called stress 'the health epidemic of the 21st Century' has recently stated that 'depression is the leading cause of ill health and disability worldwide' and also, even more worryingly, predicts that by 2030 'there will be more people affected by depression than any other health problem'. Regardless of the costs of this, shown below, surely the biggest concern is the human effect this has on the individual and their families. Almost 40% of employees believe 'it is impossible to maintain a fast-growing career and a sound family life,' thanks to the 'work-martyr' effect in companies.[17] There can be no excuse for a 'blind eye' to this.

The 'WHO' estimate that workplace stress is costing US businesses over $300 billion a year and an EU funded study[18] in 2013 estimated that the cost to employers in Europe of workplace depression was in excess of €510 billion, comprised of the costs of absenteeism and 'presenteeism' of €272 billion and €242 billion in lost productivity.

This word 'presenteeism' is a word invented to explain the phenomenon of feeling the need to be at work when suffering an illness, or feeling the need to be seen to be working long hours 'because that's what's expected of you as an employee'. To put this new phenomenon into context, Professor Sir Cary Cooper, Professor of Organization Psychology at the UK's Manchester Business School, in his speech to the CIPD Annual Conference in 2015, quoted by People Management,[19] estimates 'the cost of presenteeism to be twice the cost of absenteeism'.

Have We Learnt Nothing?

Surely by now we've realized that overlong working hours are detrimental to our health and the wellbeing of the businesses we work for. There's probably over a century of research that confirms that it is bad for our health and bad for the organizations who demand it of us. And, to compound our health concerns, if we think that extending the working day by working while at home as opposed to the office might be better for us, a recent scientific study in the UK and reported in the Sunday Times, showed that 'dealing with work issues while at home is pernicious to health and directly linkable to cardiovascular disease'.

For those who think this will all be solved when the rapidly ageing baby Boomers finally quit the workforce and leave it to the Millennials, think again. A report by the American Psychological Association[20] in 2015 found that Millennials had the highest stress levels of all the generations. So, the problems of stress and depression aren't going away anytime soon!

What those at the top of organizations don't seem to get still, after all the above, is that the culture they set pervades the organization and is having an undesirable effect on their workforce, their levels of productivity and therefore the organization's bottom line, let alone the cost to their reputation, as web-based sites like Glassdoor will expose. We are witnessing a vicious circle of greater pressure on employees through 24/7 accessibility, leading to longer hours, disengagement and presenteeism, which in turn reduces productivity, which leads to zero wage increases, further disengagement and so down and down we go in a self-defeating spiral with depression waiting for us at the bottom.

In 2008, Harvard Business Review (HBR) conducted a survey[21] of people in professional service companies (accountants, lawyers, consultants, investment bankers, IT workers, etc.). The results showed that 94% of 1000 such professionals worked 50 or more hours a week, with nearly half that group turning in more than 65 hours a week. That doesn't include the 20–25 hours a week most of them spend monitoring their BlackBerrys while outside the office. These individuals further say they almost always respond within an hour of receiving a message from a colleague or a client. Not a recipe for continuing high levels of engagement.

Such is the expectation of professional service. Work comes first, above all else. Whatever the deleterious effects on employees, their home life, their health, the expectations are that wherever you are, you are expected to be reachable.

However, HBR then conducted research with the Boston Consulting Group (BCG) and their consultants around planned, predictable time off. The research, over multiple years in several North American offices of BCG suggests that it is perfectly possible for consultants and other professionals to meet the highest standards of service and still have planned, uninterrupted time off. Indeed, the results demonstrated that when the assumption that everyone needs to be always available was collectively challenged, not only could individuals take time off, but their work actually benefited. The experiments with time off resulted in more open dialogue among team members, which is valuable in itself. But the improved communication also sparked new processes that enhanced the teams' ability to work most efficiently and effectively.

Compared with those not participating in the experiments, people on time-off teams reported higher job satisfaction, greater likelihood that they could imagine a long-term career at the firm, and higher satisfaction with work/life balance.

Is It Any Wonder Levels of Engagement Aren't Improving?

Since the seminal book on engagement, 'The Service Profit Chain'[22] was written in 1997, the link between employee engagement, customer satisfaction and loyalty, revenue growth and profitability has been well established. Statistics from Gallup,[23] the leaders in this field, who have been conducting research for over 20 years, in their 2016 'Meta Q12'™ analysis of 1.8 million employees across 73 countries, confirms the 'true relationship between engagement and performance at the business unit level, including customer loyalty, productivity, revenue and profitability', as do similar studies by Aon Hewitt, the other major player in this field.

Surely, Most Companies Run 'Satisfaction Surveys Now?

If this is the case, why do so many organizations not embrace employee engagement as a critical factor in improving their business results? A surprising 18% of companies do not use any form of engagement survey.[24] While many organizations will answer, 'we do', why is that the overall survey results from Gallup show 'only 13% of employees worldwide are actively engaged and 24% are actively disengaged'?

Sometimes the answer is that lip service is paid to employee satisfaction. Companies will tell you it is a key focus. Employees will tell you they only focus on the company needs, not what is important to them as employees and that no real meaningful actions are ever taken as a result of surveys. Equally, the rise of the expectation of 24/7 accessibility and that an employee's time is there to be abused if the company feels the need, are just as likely to be prime issues. Add to this the continuing ratcheting up of demands on employees, causing a rise in workplace and home stress. Have you ever seen an athlete or a sportsman give their best when they were stressed? No, they may be 'in the zone', but that's not being stressed. Research by McKinsey[25] has shown that workplace incivility arising from workplace stress is increasing and had been reported by 62% of those surveyed. The impacts reported as a result of this incivility, most often included a fall-off in performance and collaboration, plus an effect on customer relations and leaving intentions. Employees also see the continuing flattening of their pay levels while the 'top dogs' continue to enjoy huge multiples of average employee earnings and watch them get paid off handsomely when they inevitably fail. Of all the company's various stakeholders (shareholders, society, customers, employees, suppliers and Governments) it will be employees who will be the first to feel any ill winds.

You Need to Take Responsibility

At this time, all the benefits of technology have gone to help organizations increase their grip on us. So far, all we've got out of it is Facebook, Snapchat and Twitter, oh and people working on the potential for fridges that tell us we've run out of milk. The 'March of the Robots', as A.I. begins to replace workers with machines, will be yet another attack on employees. And, don't hold your breath waiting for society/governments to come up with solutions to these issues. By the time that happens all the value will have been taken by the few, yet again.

You can read later in this book what needs to be done to redress the balance to ensure your employees aren't part of the disaffected masses.

What not to do to raise engagement levels.

Here is an example of misusing digital technology, resulting in both a poor outcome to the initiative and managing to kill engagement. Carole Stevenson, Founder of Cybéle, a world-wide Training Consultancy, reports that a major company in the financial services sector took the decision to switch to 95% e-learning and mobile learning, with just 5% face to face learning. The expectation was that the digital learning would be done whilst travelling, which would result in cost and time saving, and deliver the upskilling while requiring less involvement from managers. The reality was different—little acceptance of this 'one size fits all' standalone digital learning and the imposition on employees' time, combined with the lack of support and dialogue and social learning required. Result: no real changes in behavior, mind-set or skill levels and really poor engagement.

'Gig', or Contingent Workers

One emerging trend is the rise of 'gig' or contingent workers. The term includes freelancers, independent professionals and contractors who are not employed directly by the company they are working for. The rise in the numbers of these workers can be attributed to a number of factors: the ability that digital technology has provided for people to work remotely in a number of professions; the need for companies to have people working on specific projects for a defined period of time; and not least, the continuing need for companies to lower their fixed employee costs. Different to the past, gig workers are more often than not highly skilled, specialized knowledge workers. The worldwide web is awash with websites that allow companies to search for the skills they need and for the workers to advertise their capabilities and find the work they are seeking.

My Choice or Yours?

Clearly for some 'giggers', this is a welcome choice, allowing them to be free from the 'tyranny' of being employed, giving them freedom to choose where and when they work. For others, it is a forced move, caused by there not being an employed position available. The 2016 EY survey[26] on the 'gig economy' in the USA found that only just over 50% would prefer not to be employed full-time, leaving a vast rump who are there because they can't find a better alternative. These workers have a real chance of becoming the new 'precariat'. The 'precariat' are simply defined as 'existing without predictability or security'. Even though employment is never guaranteed by the employer, it often provides an employee with a much greater feeling of security, particularly if that individual has a family to support and/or a mortgage to pay. This is the group of people that political parties are recognizing need to be protected from the ravages of the new order brought on by the changing nature of the world of work. The issues faced by these workers are very different to those for whom gigging is their preferred choice. However, there is real, and growing concern of the societal impact such a disaffected group could have. If companies cut their numbers of employees to reduce costs and take on gig workers in their place, then more people will be forced into this way of working against their will. Inevitably, this will increase calls for these workers to be granted some form of employment benefits, including holidays, sick pay and pension rights. If Governments feel that they are losing revenue in the form of taxes through the rise of gig workers, expect them to support these calls.

Even with the significant increase that has taken place so far, further expansion is forecast. The EY survey (above) says that 1/3 of the companies with over 100,000 employees expect to have over 30% of contingent workers by 2020 and other forecasts suggest a 50/50 share is the most likely long term future outcome.

Disengagement for All?

It is unlikely to be plain sailing. In an HBR article,[27] quoting research by Rosalind Bergemann, 74% of contract workers left employment because of 'lack of employer engagement'. So companies need to ensure that the environment they provide does switch them on, or they will be as dissatisfied gigging for the new 'boss' as they were for their previous employer. This is only one of the major emerging issues that business leaders will face. Concerns include ensuring that these workers are properly inducted into the organization's culture, the style of operating and to oversee the full transfer of knowledge to the organization. If project workers are to be based alongside employees, then ensuring the operating style and culture set by the organization is adhered to by the project worker is vital. Underestimating the need to closely manage the progress of a project team and the subsequent transfer of their knowledge into the organization is a real danger. Too often this isn't the case and the project team are allowed to operate as if on a different planet. A quote from an Agile team leader of over 30 giggers on a major systems project said 'there is little or no ownership by management and we don't see anyone from the beginning of the one week to the end. They won't know what to do with our project when it's delivered as they're not involved enough.' While this individual wishes to remain anonymous, he also stresses that this project is little different to others he's been involved in.

If these workers are spending time at the same workplace as employees, and aren't operating to the same demands, standards, culture then the adverse effect on employees' motivation will be significant. These workers have 'no skin in the game', so the long term success of the organization means little or nothing to them beyond being paid for their time. Employees who see others 'getting away with it', will have little confidence in the leadership's ability to develop a successful organization. While, clearly, individual contractors are more likely to have their reputation at stake, they are, in theory, only as good as their last assignment. As always though, references are only one of the many checks that need to be performed as companies tend to gloss over issues once the assignment is complete.

To make a success of using this new band of skilled workers requires an approach that recognizes the needs of the different individuals and groups. Anything less than the time and effort that would have been applied if they were employees, risks projects running over budget and time. It also risks the real disaffection of those who carry the organization day in, week in and year in and out: the hard-pressed, increasingly hard done by employees.

Multitasking

If only we were all educated, energetic and eager Millennials, capable of performing three tasks simultaneously while posting on Snapchat… Or, actually, no STOP THERE! Because in reality it's about about the worst thing we could do. Already there is a wealth of evidence available that tells us just how bad multitasking is both for us as individuals and the organizations for which we work. The overarching tyranny of the digital world has taken us to a place where we allow every ping, ding or buzz to pull us away from what we were doing. We sit with multiple apps/websites open, inviting those distractions. A study by Gloria Mark of the University of California, quoted in the New York Times,[28] concluded it took a full 25 min to properly refocus ourselves once our attention had been diverted.

There have been plenty other studies. A Stanford University study[29] demonstrated that typical single-taskers outperformed regular multitaskers in a range of tasks; the University of London, quoted in Forbes,[30] conducted tests that showed multitasking recorded a drop of 15 IQ points, equivalent to the effect of having gone without sleep for a night.

There's also research from the UK's Sussex University, quoted in EurekAlert[31] in 2014 that suggests there is potential long-term damage to the area of the brain responsible for EQ (emotional intelligence) from multitasking. That could presage that we will be working in really unpleasant workplaces in the future! Unhappy and underperforming, doesn't begin to cover the future's possibilities.

How Big Did You Say?

But the most significant survey is this one. Realization, a major US Project Management services company, performed an extensive survey of 45 companies across a wide range of industries and examined numerous academic studies in their 2013 report 'The Effect of Multitasking on Organizations'[32]. From this, they estimated that the loss in productivity arising from knowledge workers multitasking is around $450 billion a year globally! That truly shows the economic value that we are losing by this pernicious influence.

And if you're still inclined to think that this is overstated, just think of texting while driving a car. Or, maybe you prefer the old Roman proverb: 'a man who chases two rabbits catches none' (World of Proverbs).

What's becoming clear is that it is making more practical sense than ever to focus on the task at hand and leave the rest until a natural break stage arises where you would have stopped anyway. For leaders, there is a huge need to set this example and, by doing this, encourage all others to do the same.

Key Learnings for Leaders

It is different this time. It's not the same as the 'pressures we've always experienced'. Smartphones and 24/7 accessibility have hugely exacerbated and transformed the demands on employees. You cannot continue to lead as if nothing has changed.

The employee backlash from unreasonable demands is growing, as the requirement to be 'always on' is abused and the benefits of success go only to a few. You need to act on 'macho management'.

Continuing low levels of employee engagement are costing organizations billions of dollars, euros and yen a year. Are you even trying to meet employees' legitimate expectations?

Email has become an invasive infection threatening the health of organizations with no real antidote in sight. This will only change if you, as leaders, take action.

Rise in workplace stress and depression is already at epidemic levels, costing billions and receiving insufficient leadership focus. Your employees' well-being is your responsibility.

Gig workers require the same attention as your employees or you won't get value from them and they could pollute the organization. Make sure you know how to manage them.

The number of potential distractions during the working day deflect hugely from the concentrated effort required to add real value and are having a huge impact on organizations' productivity. If you don't take action on this nobody else will.

3

Why it's a Business Issue

Alain Haut and Peter Thomson

Technology is impacting organizations of all sizes, but many leaders are acting as if it's still 'business as usual'. Digitalization needs to be addressed at senior level as a strategy to avoid problems such as overload. Human capital must be maintained as a critical asset, contributing to business success.

Overview

We are living in a digital age. No business, large or small, can avoid the effect of technology on the way their operation is run, their relationship with customers and the markets they can address. It is not just businesses

A. Haut (✉)
FutureWork Forum, Geneva, Switzerland
e-mail: alain.haut@oplc.ch

P. Thomson
FutureWork Forum, Henley-on-Thames, UK
e-mail: peter.thomson@me.com

© The Author(s) 2018
P. Thomson et al. (eds.), *Conquering Digital Overload*,
https://doi.org/10.1007/978-3-319-63799-0_3

in the technology sector that are impacted. 'Digitalization' varies by sector and by size of organization. It also varies between countries.

Recent credible research[33] has concluded that the USA has reached a level of 63% of digitalization potential in business, based on current available digitalization applications, closely followed by emerging countries (59%) while overall, the world of business has reached 41% of digitalization potential. Europe is trailing but hopefully catching up.

Three Categories of Digital Experience

Our own research suggests three broad categories of experience with digital technology.

The *digital collaboration experience* (including social collaboration and intranet strategies, increase in staff productivity, mobile digital workplace and knowledge management) focuses on IT, communications, knowledge, social media and mobile support staff.

The *digital customer experience* (including customer expectations in the digital age, cross-channel customer service, digital marketing, strategies in business-to-consumer very often, and business-to-business more rarely, content marketing and customer relations analytics …). This concerns marketing and commercial executives and experts.

The *digital change and engagement experience* (including social and digital learning, employees' engagement, cultural transformation and digital team leading). This addresses the concerns of senior leadership that the overall approach is cohesive and that employees are able to maximise the potential benefits.

The Size and Scope of the Problem

Add these together and we have a huge challenge to build a corporate digital culture. We need to gain the benefits of digital processes in the business without the problems. However, there are many organisations, large and small, that have just allowed the technology to enter the business without a planned approach. Applications have been introduced without consideration of the impact on the rest of the business. Existing working practices have remained in place and not been adapted to the digital age. Applications like email have been introduced without any consideration of the impact they have on other communications channels.

The problem is that 'digital' is seen as something that is handled by the IT department. It is not considered a leadership issue. This is compounded by the fact that many leaders worked their way to the top in a pre-digital era. Their understanding of their business, and the way people work in it, is conditioned by their own experience. Some are technophobes who are not personally comfortable with using new applications in their working lives. They may delay the introduction of new technologies but will generally be convinced by a financial argument. They will probably accept individual proposals which result in a piecemeal approach to digitalization.

Where is the Strategy?

If there is no digital strategy and it is simply a series of disjointed applications, there are bound to be problems. Overlap, duplication and wasted resources are obvious results. But the most critical is the impact on employee workload. If new technologies are introduced they should be replacing old ones. With specific applications this happens. The new computerised accounting system replaces manual bookkeeping effort. The new product database replaces the old paper based inventory system. Automating the employee records reduces HR admin effort.

But what happens when email is introduced; what is this replacing? What is the effect of introducing a video conferencing facility; does the number of meetings go down or up? What is the benefit having an Intranet; is there a saving in effort somewhere? A company website is likely an imperative for all, but how is the additional work of keeping it up-date and relevant to be maintained?

Without an integrated approach to the digitization of work it is likely to be counterproductive. Instead of reducing workload, it increases it. Instead of bringing clarity to communications, it confuses it. And instead of simplifying life, it complicates it.

This is the nub of the digital overload problem. The new technologies have been simply overlaid on the old working methods without any consideration of the impact. They have been introduced in isolation without looking at the effect they have on the individual. Giving someone email as a tool is fine, as long as they can use it to improve the way they work. If it simply adds an additional task of clearing an overloaded inbox each day, then it is a burden not a help. Giving someone a video-conferencing facility is only useful if it substitutes effectively for some face-to-face meetings and saves people having to waste time on travel.

Taking an overview of the complete business is a key leadership function. Being able to see the impact of the digital revolution on the whole organisation is critical. Understanding how to adapt to the new opportunities and threats should be at the top of the agenda for the leadership team. Staying competitive may well depend on beating the competition by using technology to reduce costs, increase responsiveness or even create whole new product families.

It's a Leadership Issue!

Operational issues concerned with the use of technology may be delegated to the experts but the purpose and strategy cannot be. Here are six 'dimensions' that need to be considered at senior level:

- *From inside and isolated to connected performance improvement*
  Digitization is not just happening inside the organization. It has an impact on the relationship with customers, suppliers and contractors. How is it contributing to the bottom line, the workforce, the market and society?
- *From individual winners and losers to collective cooperation*
  Does the technology just help some people to perform more effectively or does it have wider impact? Can it help teams work more effectively?
- *From stability (leading to stagnation?) to start-up entrepreneurial approach*
  Can the technology create new products, services and markets?
- *From functional protection to innovation for all, leading to autonomy*
  Digital applications can be used to reinforce existing stovepipes or can help break them down. They support an innovative culture for people to introduce new ideas.

- *From controlled knowledge to pragmatic increased knowledge*
  Manipulation of data (big data) is a powerful tool for the organization but only if the knowledge is shared. Leaders have to reward sharing of knowledge and discourage the hoarding of information for political reasons.
- *From burn-outs and lay-offs to new jobs, transparency and work-life balance*
  Technology can have a negative effect on job satisfaction, leading to employee demotivation and increased turnover. Smart use of technology should both attract and help motivate employees, particularly if also backed up by life-long training in the application.

This final dimension is the focus for this book. We know that there is an increase in stress levels associated with the use of digital technologies. We have 'long hours cultures' causing burn-out and low productivity. And we know that all organisations, regardless of sector, aim to get the best value for money from their workforce. The most important job for the senior management team is to achieve the goals of the organisation in the most cost-effective way, not just in the short term but in the medium to long timescale.

Technology is now capable of taking over the routine tasks from people. Robots have replaced production-line workers and computers have replaced paper-pushers in the office. What is left should therefore be the more interesting parts of the old jobs. We should be able to design work processes that are less stressful and more fulfilling. We should be creating new jobs that tap into human creativity and are rewarding for the individuals involved.

Instead, we have work patterns that invade individual's personal lives and organisation cultures that encourage an 'always on' behaviour. We have workloads that result in low productivity and increased errors, because people are working when they are tired. We are seeing an increase in ill-health and absenteeism amongst staff. Why is this?

The answer is that senior managers have not recognised that this is a business issue. Or if they have recognised it, they don't have a viable approach to changing it. That is until a competitor comes up with an answer that forces them to. They have not made a conscious decision to manage the organisational culture, they have let it evolve. They have left 'digitalization' decisions to someone down in the IT department and they have left employee welfare to a junior HR person. Because it is difficult to measure the effectiveness of the workforce they have allowed the 'human resource' to work inefficiently and not maintained it as a vital resource.

We invest in capital equipment and run it within specified limits. We would not deliberately run machinery above maximum speed/capacity knowing that it will break down as a result. We will carry out the routine maintenance on equipment so it will work effectively and reliably. But when it comes to the human resource we throw out these sensible guidelines and allow it to overload. To further exacerbate the problem, senior management set an example of long hours working which encourages unhealthy working patterns.

Investing in human capital and using it productively is a key business goal. But it is one that often drops down the gap between the chairs around the boardroom table. The HR Director may have responsibility for attracting and retaining people. The Finance Director may be looking at the labour costs in the profit and loss account. Operational directors may be worried about achieving their goals with the resources at their disposal. But who is responsible for maximising the productivity of the workforce as a whole?

Keeping the skills of the workforce up to date and equipping people for the jobs of the future is both a leadership responsibility and a government challenge. Organisations will need to play their part in training people in the skills needed for the next digital age. And it will also become a critical issue for governments to ensure that they have the intellectual resources in the population to fill the new jobs. In 1931, Keynes was already analysing the risk of 'technology unemployment' but so far we have found that as old jobs disappeared, new ones replaced them. Overall, employment was maintained and even grew.

It Doesn't Work Anymore

But the tendency from government and unions has been to prop up dying industries such as coal and steel to maintain employment for as long as possible. Now, old sectors are disappearing so rapidly and new ones emerging that the approach has to change. Instead of maintaining outdated skills, governments and industries will have to work together to develop the capabilities needed in the digital economy. It cannot be left to the 'gig economy' to develop the competencies of the working population.

Increases in stress levels are concrete evidence that something has gone wrong with today's working practices. Senior managers are blindly continuing to run twentieth century operations despite the fact that we are well into the twenty first century. Someone at board level has to grasp the nettle and ask the question 'What kind of organisation do we want to be?' Do we want to have people working 50–60 hours per week because that's the way you impress your boss? Or do we want to have people who go home early because they've found a way to get the job done in less time? What behaviour do we want to reward and how do we get that message through the organisation? How should we as the leaders set the example?

Another key business question is 'How do we get work done?' The traditional answer to this is that we employ people, typically in full-time jobs, pay them salaries and offer them career opportunities. Increasingly this approach is being questioned.

Could the work be done by someone outside the organisation, either a supplier or an individual self-employed contractor? If it makes sense to employ someone does it have to be a full-time job? Does the work have to be done at fixed times or could the person choose? Can some work be done remotely? Is the position permanent or is there a foreseeable time when it goes away?

We have recently seen a series of reports about the potential for jobs to be replaced with technology. We cover more about this in the last chapter of this book as we look into the future. There is speculation that up to 50% of all jobs will disappear in the next 20–30 years and there will not be enough work to go around. What work there is will be spread more thinly. So people will not have to take on jobs that fit into a five day week. They will probably work shorter hours. Combined with the need for people to stay working into their 60s and 70s we will see the demand rise for part-time work.

Good leaders are aware of what is happening in the world around them. They need to take into account the social and demographic trends. They need now to break out from the traditional view of work based on the 40 hour week and think about alternatives. Many people would like to work shorter hours but they are stuck in full-time jobs. They will vote with their feet if employers don't respond.

At the 2016 Davos Forum, there was a consensus around the loss of 5 million jobs by 2020 due to automation and digitalization around the world, with the obvious most dramatic impact on western and developed economies. A similar conclusion came from the 2016 OECD report[34] which concluded that there is more than 70% of risk that an average of 10% of jobs could be totally eliminated through automation. They also predicted that an additional 25% of jobs, although not substituted entirely, will however 'suffer' a significant (50+%) elimination of some of the tasks.

These are changes that cannot be ignored by business leaders. Working lives will never be the same. Employees can expect to see their work function changing fundamentally every three years. They are likely to change employer every 7–8 years. Over a 45 year career an average employee will have 15 different work functions and 6–7 different employers. And for most of those jobs we can't predict what they will be.

We are also seeing more predictions about the 'Gig Economy' and the proliferation of independent entrepreneurs. One of the drivers that will accelerate this process is the need for people to have more control over the way they work. If people are stressed out by the traditional job, they are likely to opt for self-employment to rebalance their lives. Organisations that stick with a traditional employment model are likely to lose their talent to those that are more agile.

The 'Millennials' joining the workforce are expecting to integrate their job into the rest of their lives. They are not happy to have to adapt their personal activities to fit around a fixed pattern of work. They have grown up with digital tools at their convenience in the rest of their lives, so they assume they are there at work. Why should they spend all day in boring meetings in the office when they could be collaborating with an information-sharing app? Why can't they choose to work at times they are most effective not at times dictated by their boss? Why do they have to work excessively long hours in a low productivity environment when they know a smarter way to get the job done which only takes half the time?

Same End Game, But How You Get There Has Changed

Attracting and retaining the best people is a critical part of business strategy. Talent management is not just something delegated to the HR function. It's the responsibility of the board to build and maintain a productive workforce. They set the culture of the organization and they need to actively manage it. They are responsible for the policies and processes that govern people's working lives. Ultimately, every board decision can have an impact on the satisfaction and engagement felt by an employee. And this directly impacts the output from that individual.

We cover engagement in more detail in a later chapter, but it is important to emphasize it here as a strategic issue. So often it is seen as 'keeping the employees happy' and a 'soft' measure in the business. But there is ample evidence to prove that productivity is directly related to engagement. Employees who feel appreciated and rewarded in their work will produce more, collaborate better and stay longer. It therefore makes sense for senior management to look carefully at the working environment and create an engaging culture. The success of any business depends on the effectiveness of the workforce.

Maintaining a healthy workforce is of strategic importance. In the past the HR function has run the 'wellbeing' program, typically providing subsidized gym membership and counselling services. But what's the point of providing gym membership when people can't find the time to take exercise anyway? Why is there a need to provide counselling services; it's because people are suffering from stress. We are good at dealing with the symptoms. What leadership needs to do is tackle the source of the problem.

There may be many causes of work related stress, but there is one that we see around us on a daily basis. This is the intrusion of technology into our lives, the 24/7 culture that keeps us 'at work' wherever we are.

But it's not the technology itself that is causing the stress, it's the way it is being imposed on people. If it is added on to the existing pattern of work it can quickly become an extra burden. It is substitutes for an outdated working practice then it becomes liberating. So dealing with the problem by throttling the technology is not the answer.

Some organisations have however taken this approach. They 'suspend' e-mails and/or professional internet/device connections outside work hours. In 2012, VW in Canada was switching off internet access by employees half an hour after end of work time and only switching on half an hour before start of work time. Recently, Kedge Business School (the merged school between two top level French 'Grandes Ecoles De Commerce' of Marseille and Bordeaux) was very proud to announce their strict application, for both faculty and students, of the same system as described for VW Canada.

Just turning off the technology is dealing with the symptoms not the problem. It is taking a 'we know best' approach and is the direct opposite of an engaging culture. It makes the assumption that everyone works the regular 'opening hours' and work should not be done outside of this time. This cancels out all the positive messages about empowering employees and giving them control over their own lives. And all it does is to allow the emails to build up over the offline time and still be there when eventually the system comes back on.

This paternalistic attitude toward employees also extends to government decisions. The right to disconnect has become a much talked about subject since it became a legal obligation in France. It has had a mixed reaction both negatively (legal interference in the right to work) and positively (once more, we are pioneers in improving work conditions). Employers who resort to the legislation to make their decisions for them are not showing leadership on this issue. They need to tackle the source of the problem, the organizational culture.

Despite many efforts by academics, consultants and business philosophers (they cannot be all wrong!), business leaders continue to apply, to a very great extent, the 'traditional way of managing': planning, physical proximity, directive leadership, centralized hierarchy, silo culture, control and limited delegation, risk averse processes, set parameters (time, space etc.), closed system and traditional business fundamentals (capital, cash-flow, information, knowledge).

On the other hand, the 'new way of managing' favours different approaches: adaptation, blended work (site and distance), negotiation and consensus, transversal decentralization, cooperation between individuals and departments, autonomy and trust, the right to make mistakes, very limited risk parameters, open systems, and fast reactions to short-term projects.

Business leaders tend to be risk averse. Consequently they will stick with what they know to be safe and will not easily make changes, particularly where the results are not clearly quantified. So they may be comfortable with digitalization where it clearly brings efficiencies but may not understand the behavioural implications of some technologies. They may approve the use of a mobile app without thinking through the impact it has on someone's personal life. Top managers have a social responsibility to run an organization that does not burn people out. They must embrace the digital age by understanding the changes that it brings, good and bad, and consciously manage the culture.

Here's the Leadership Challenge

Because of this this new managerial approach, leaders must acquire and develop new competencies:

- Social and relational intelligence (network)
- Novel and adaptive thinking
- Cross-cultural (diversity/inclusion) thinking
- Computational thinking (big data)
- Conceptual thinking
- New media literacy
- A holistic cross-discipline approach
- Ability to organize virtual cooperation
- Mental flexibility
- Curiosity, intuition, creativity
- Criticality, selection and focus
- Balance between work and mental load

And this implies that business leaders with those competencies respect their employees' sense of privacy, ownership, consumption, work/leisure balance, career/skills development and relationships.

Leaders also have the responsibility for setting an example to the rest of the workforce. They may suggest that people should not overwork, but then work long hours themselves. They may say that people should not work at weekends, or on vacation, unless they have to, and then send emails themselves at these times. They may give the impression that it's 'OK' to have a good life/work balance and then be clearly seen to work excessive hours themselves. The message here is clear; 'If you want to get on in this organization follow my example, don't listen to what I say'.

Managers themselves are not immune from overload. Some recent research[35] at Henley Business School showed that 92% of managers work longer than their contracted hours. 61% also say that technology has made it difficult to switch off from work. They are constantly interrupted by the phone causing symptoms similar to ADHD. This study of 'technostress' shows that managers in their 40s and 50s are much more likely to be distracted by the interruptions then those in their 20s and 30s. In contrast, managers in the 45–54 age bracket are the least likely to feel invaded by the technology.

Managers over 50 are more likely to feel their job security threatened by technology than their younger counterparts but are less likely to think that the technology improves their performance. These results are not surprising, however the research did show one interesting anomaly. Role Overload is not directly related to performance, although it does have significant relationship with job security. The more technology invades home life the more people feel their performance goes up, but when Role Overload is average to high it reduces perceptions of the positive impact of technology on performance.

So managers and leaders should be avoiding digital overload for the benefit of their own performance as well as setting a good example for others. If they are measuring their own performance on the basis of output, not input, they will show that high performers are the people who get the job done in the shortest time. They will be seen going home early and having a less stressful existence. They will push back on the 'macho' culture that brags about long hours and low productivity.

They will empower their people to manage their own work patterns and will trust them to work in the way that suits them best. And they will be running successful businesses, harnessing the power of digital technology rather than being overwhelmed by it.

Conclusion

The speed of the change which digital technology has enabled, has caught many organisations flat-footed. It's all very well if you are a digital start-up, with no legacy systems, with millennial leadership, open to the new ways of working, but for the huge majority of established businesses, that's not the case. The danger of being left behind with a demotivated, disgruntled workforce required to work 24/7 to keep their heads above water is hugely disturbing.

The need for leadership to take ownership of the digital agenda is proven. Just as clear is the requirement on them to ensure the organisation is run in a way that empowers employees to use digital technology to free them to meet the organisation's objectives and not to enslave them.

Key Learnings for Leaders

The digital agenda is too often piecemeal and left to IT or to whoever shouts the loudest.

The potential prize, and the potential cost of failure, dictates that digital is a key leadership issue.

There are '6 Dimensions' of a digital strategy that need to be assessed.

The need to recognise the damage digital overload is doing to employees and address it is a leadership imperative.

We have focussed too much on the 'symptoms' and not addressed the 'causes' of digital overload.

Leaders need to ensure they learn and adopt new competencies.

There is a 'better way' to run organisations that will produce better results, with motivated employees, but it requires leaders to set the right example.

4

Organizational Culture, and the Impact of the Digital Overload

Ben Emmens and Peter Thomson

This chapter explores the way in which culture has been shaped by technology, and focuses on the impact technology has had on our ways of working. We will see that organizational cultures (and by extrapolation, we as individuals) are struggling to adapt to increasingly digital workplaces and are at risk of being overwhelmed by the digital overload. We identify outdated cultures which are amplified by technology. The old 'command and control' culture is being replaced a 'trust and empower' one being demanded by today's workforce.

B. Emmens (✉)
FutureWork Forum, London, UK
e-mail: ben@benemmens.com

P. Thomson
FutureWork Forum, Henley-on-Thames, UK
e-mail: peter.thomson@me.com

© The Author(s) 2018
P. Thomson et al. (eds.), *Conquering Digital Overload*,
https://doi.org/10.1007/978-3-319-63799-0_4

Introduction

Organizational culture is generally recognized as meaning the behaviors shown by employees on a daily basis, rather than the artifacts within the workplace. Of course, there are many facets of organizational culture, and others have expounded on this topic comprehensively, but for now, as we explore 'digital overload', we will take it to mean *'how things are done around here'*[36]. It's a phrase that defines culture succinctly and, in today's context, we see how culture therefore becomes inextricably bound up with technology and our theme of 'digital overload'. Culture is influenced—even defined—by both the external and the internal environment. Few, if any, organizations are able to operate in a vacuum and somehow remain oblivious to what is going on in the world around them. Political, environmental, social and technological changes have significant influence. Each plays a role in shaping culture, and what happens inside an organization is often a response to the external forces or markets.

Technology has long promised to makes things easier and faster: whether the motor car in the early 20th century, automatic washing machines in the 1950s, personal computers and cell phones in the 1980s, or platforms such as Google and Facebook in the early 21st century. However, the reality, and actual personal experience has not always matched the rhetoric. For many who live in high or middle income countries and enjoy the benefits of technology, the dark side is often an endless search for a power supply to re-charge our various devices, or being hounded by notifications at every turn, tracked by technology giants and governments alike, and targeted by advertisers who watch our every click. And it's not that different in the workplace either: a plethora of platforms, multiple devices in addition to those we own ourselves, frustrating software, mediocre software, brilliant software, databases at every turn, email and messaging systems that are always on. It's hard not to feel overwhelmed by all things digital and many workers admit technology leaves them feeling frustrated, with plenty wondering whether it was actually more productive in the good old days. According the CIPD[37] a third of employees (31%) say they come home from work exhausted either often (22%) or always (9%).

How Did We Get Here?

Although the benefits of technology are widely recognized, particularly the way in which technology can enable transparency, participation and dissemination of information, and support flexible working practices, it is also true that technology has not always been helpful. In particular, it has amplified a number of underlying factors and patterns of behavior, with the result that many organizations find themselves with a culture that is far from what they might describe as 'healthy', and perhaps not as productive as they think it is! Sometimes there is no choice to change, as today's fast moving business means that the end justifies the means, or we get swallowed by the competition.

One important factor is the way in which technology has amplified the 'long hours' culture. Of course people have been working long hours since time began, and indeed some countries such as the UK have a worse reputation than others[38] but some sectors are particularly susceptible, especially the service sector (financial and consulting) and the tech sector with its myriad internet start ups. For many of us, technology has blurred work-life boundaries and stretched the working day and working hours beyond acceptable limits. For some of course, especially working parents, technology has afforded a welcome flexibility that was previously unthinkable. But the reality is that for many of us that work, our device/s are both 'always on' and 'always with us', and outside of work, this requires a level of self-discipline beyond the reach of most people, especially when we glance at a screen and see that we have a message from the boss or a close colleague. This is supported by the UK's CIPD survey[39] which found that 15% of employees said 'they were rarely or never able to switch off from work' and 42% they were only sometimes able to do this.

It could be argued that while technology has increased 'responsiveness', it has also increased our impatience. A large proportion of the messages we receive demand an immediate acknowledgement or response: it's not unheard of for the sender of an email to also text or call the recipient to check receipt and prompt action. In many workplaces, it is the loudest voice that gets attention, and it is the swiftest response that gets recognized (and rewarded). We find ourselves drawn in, and ultimately this behavior becomes self-perpetuating: the quicker we respond, the more the expectation of a quick response increases. Not only do we find ourselves beholden to the devices that clamor for our attention, without necessarily realizing it we end up being distracted and unable to focus on important or detailed work. Thus a set of behaviors develop and over time, and they become entrenched. Our focus shifts from the important to the urgent, as this is often where the noise or pain is coming from. Moreover, as we look around, we see this repeated in various walks of life; whether the volatility of the financial markets and their immediate reaction to events, or in politics, where politicians dance to the tune of the tabloid press and their daily headlines, or elsewhere.

For sure, technology has accelerated communication. The wide availability of high speed internet access and the advent of affordable, fast mobile internet on highly portable devices are changing the world beyond recognition. In much the same way as it has fed consumerism, for example, our desire for immediate satiation has been enabled by the advent of internet based companies and services such as Amazon who with 'Amazon Prime' have made same day deliveries at an unprecedented scale at the metaphorical 'press of a button' or 'touch on a screen', technology has made it possible for us to send and receive messages instantaneously, and on any device we happen to be wearing or carrying. More than that, technology tells us when our messages have been delivered, opened and read.

Technology has not only accelerated communication, but proliferated it. The sheer amount of data we are subjected to at work on a daily basis encourages us to get to it quickly or we will drown under the weight if we leave it for another day. In itself of course, this is neither good nor bad, yet somehow, we find ourselves caught up in this frenetic world of urgent, instantaneous communication and our expectation of an immediate response has the potential to enslave both us and the recipient!

Who led us here? Did we make our own way, or are those in charge somehow responsible? Ultimately there is some degree of mutual responsibility, but it is hard to avoid the uncomfortable truth that it is those in charge, our leaders, who have the most influence in terms of shaping and setting culture. Partly, this happens through neglect, with leaders choosing to ignore the deluge of data clogging up their organization. And partly, this is done consciously when leaders believe they are benefitting from 24/7 accessibility. Even in organizations where leadership is, to a greater or lesser extent, distributed, it is those holding the most senior positions of office within a hierarchy, i.e. the leaders themselves, who end up, intentionally or otherwise, defining the culture by the example they set.

Leaders need to understand how cultural issues influence the use of digital technology. In a survey covering 1700 people in 340 organizations across eight countries and five sectors[40], Capgemini found that 62% of respondents said that culture was the number one hurdle to digital transformation. They identified three main obstacles getting in the way:

1. The leadership neglects, underestimates or misunderstands the importance of culture in their digital transformation planning.
2. The existing culture and way of doing things is so deeply ingrained that it becomes very difficult to effect change.
3. Like customers, employees too are becoming more digital.
4. Most behavioral change initiatives accomplish little because employees are not empowered to take on new challenges.

There is also a clear message to leaders coming out from this survey. While 40% of senior executives believe their organization has a digital culture, only 27% of the employees felt the same way. And 75% of senior executives believe they have a culture of innovation, but only 37% of employees feel the same. This gap has to be narrowed.

Outdated Cultures

The predominant organizational culture during the 20th Century was based on command and control. Leaders set the example, and they gave the orders. Managers down through the layers of hierarchy carried out the instructions, implemented the policies and exerted their authority. People did what they were told. Knowledge was kept as closely as possible to the seat of power and people were informed on a 'need to know' basis.

Taylorism worked well in its time. The production line brought the price of consumer goods within the grasp of the masses. People were prepared to do boring repetitive jobs in return for good pay, job security and a routine, predictable lifestyle. Corporate cultures reflected society, with a tacit acceptance of levels of authority, often reflecting a class structure in the national culture. Social mobility was limited, as was career progression. The model of work was based on full time male employment and very limited opportunities for women.

Fast forward to the 21st Century and what do we have? Social change has been dramatic. The role of women in western cultures has largely shifted from stay-at-home mother to equal partner at work. Equal rights have been enshrined within legislation and diversity is encouraged. The balance between work and the rest of life has shifted and flexibility in work patterns is rapidly becoming the norm. Society is becoming more tolerant of people who don't fit the stereotypical norm, from race and color to sexual orientation and religious beliefs.

Yet, many organizational cultures look more like they are still in the 20th Century, or even the 19th. This is hardly surprising. Who is it that chooses the leaders of our major companies or our government departments? It's the existing leadership. They nurture and promote people who support the status quo. To challenge the way things are being done is to be a trouble-maker or a rebel. So there is an inbuilt inertia in any culture that ignores changes happening in the outside world until they are materially affecting the business or are imposed by legislation.

Governments have had to recognize that social change is happening and force it on employers through legislation. Equal rights based on race and gender are common across major industrialized nations but many organizations have struggled to comply with them. The current debate about quotas for women on the boards of companies illustrates the need for external pressures or intervention in order for change to happen. An instance of this is the fact that The Times in the UK publishes an annual report on 'the top 50 employers for women in the UK'. Surely this is a clear sign that our work cultures have not kept up with the rhetoric. Despite legislation in some countries giving rights to request flexible working, there are still outdated assumptions by some managers and leaders that all work has to be full-time and at a fixed location.

Even without the additional factor of today's technology we would still find ourselves experiencing outdated leadership cultures. Add 'digital' to the mix and we have amplified the issue to the point where it can no longer be ignored. The old 'command and control' culture has to give way to a 'trust and empower' one that better reflects the needs and aspirations of today's workforce. Organizations will not be able to attract and retain the best people if they refuse to adapt to new ways of working. Already we are seeing a substantial number of professionals voting with their feet and quitting the corporate rat-race. Quality of life is winning over high pay and career progression.

This is particularly true of the Millennial generation. They typically expect to have freedom to work in a way that suits their personal life-style. They have grown up with digital technology that allows them to manage their personal life. So they expect to have control over their working life. They assume they will be trusted by their managers to get the job done without someone constantly looking over their shoulder. They will respect their managers and leaders when those same managers and leaders have earned it. They certainly don't respond well to incompetent leaders just because they have positions of authority in the hierarchy.

It is often the leaders who continue to set a poor example. Often baby boomers, these are men who started their working life at a time when people were more willing to sacrifice personal life on the altar of corporate careers, and many have found it hard to adapt and change their working approaches and assumptions. Even if they recognize that times have changed, they have difficulty changing their own personal habits. They didn't get where they are today by taking time off for parental leave or by working part time. So why should the next generation? They may reluctantly accept that flexible working is becoming commonplace further down in the organization, but of course to be a director or senior level executive involves working unsocial hours and being constantly on call. It's not surprising that with this male-oriented working model there is a glass ceiling for anyone wanting a balanced life.

For the last 50 years we have been told by a succession of management gurus that the way to get the best out of people is to trust them and treat them like adults. Yet many corporate cultures are still essentially Taylorist by nature. They impose rules on people for their own good. They give people detailed job descriptions so they can follow the system consistently. They implement 'quality' programs to ensure everything is done in a uniform and predictable way. They reward loyalty to the status quo and obedience to the rules. And they add layer upon layer of management structures, adding bureaucracy and stifling initiative.

So, the freedom that is provided by digital technology is ignored. Instead of the smartphone giving an employee more control over how they do their job, it simply extends the hours they are working. Instead of levelling the playing field between the part-time and full-time worker it accentuates the difference. Instead of bringing autonomy and freedom it has invaded people's lives and dominated their time. Technology is not the problem. It is a catalyst that highlights the issue of outdated cultures and poor leadership. It amplifies the culture that surrounds it. It allows authoritarian managers to exercise control and micro-manage.

A Plethora of Platforms

Today's workers typically find themselves interacting with a wide range of digital platforms, often simultaneously. Often heralded as the successor to the ubiquitous email, platforms offer levels of functionality and customization that email simply cannot compete with. By the broadest definition 'platform' includes a wide range of web based applications that enable collaborative work and communication. At the last count, the author's desktop, tablet and smartphone were running twitter, LinkedIn, Slack, Basecamp 2 and 3, Skype, WhatsApp, Box, Dropbox, Google Docs, and Skype. You may use Facebook, SharePoint, and, quite likely, your company's in-house Yammer to add to the profusion, as well as many others.

Platforms, document sharing applications and instant messaging services may come and go, but despite one or two examples of companies that have tried to do away with email, sadly no platform has replaced the ubiquitous email. The real challenge with platforms is the sheer number of them. Each has its fans and detractors and it is not uncommon for an organization to adopt a number of them, thus eliminating many of the potential efficiency benefits that were promised.

Like email, and often through the medium of email, platforms have a way of competing for our constant attention and immediate interaction. It is the relentless bombardment from email and messaging services which combine to put today's organizations and us, the individuals within them, under enormous and unyielding pressure.

The Myth of Multi-Tasking

Much has been written about multi-tasking: some can, some can't; entirely possible, entirely impossible; and so forth. With respect to technology, the ability to multi-task effectively is almost certainly a myth. Try having a conversation with a teenager who is messaging friends on WhatsApp, or playing Minecraft, or think back to your last conference call and how successfully you juggled participation and active-listening with other tasks on your to do list! It's not just that it's hard. In some contexts it's considered impossible or even illegal to multi-task, for example driving a vehicle and using a hand-held cellphone is a criminal offence, and other research has suggested having a phone conversation (hands-free) whilst driving is equivalent to driving under the influence of alcohol[41]. Yet we persist with the belief that we can be productive while doing several tasks at once, usually aided and abetted by some technological support.

Generational Perspectives?

To what extent do generational differences (or for that matter cultural differences) influence our digital perspective, and sense of digital overload?

Like the apocryphal frog in the boiling water (who fails to jump out as the water slowly reaches boiling point, and thus meets an untimely demise), many have experienced nothing other than being immersed in an increasingly digital world that is 'always on', and, whether knowingly or unknowingly, our world is being comprehensively digitized. Smart telephones and smart televisions, intelligent assistants and artificial intelligence, always on internet and a life ruled by algorithms: children and young people growing up in the west are having to adapt rapidly. Our ability to adapt and cope with change typically comes less easily as we grow older. In workplaces where we have four or five generations the possibilities for misunderstanding and confusion are plentiful, and frequent.

Intuitively we say it is easier for the younger generations to adopt the latest technology and adapt, and for those that are working, often the technology they have in their pocket is vastly superior to that which their employer can provide. Technology seems to be guilty of driving on the one hand individualization (picture many individual hunched over their phones) and on the other hand hyper-connectedness. This paradox is proving a real challenge for organizations to overcome, and the resultant organizational culture is fragile, and sometimes shallow. For where relationships are mediated by a screen and a swipe, who has the patience to do the long hard and slow work of trust-building? It's not always possible to tell who's at the other end either.

Networked thinking and networked working presents both opportunities and risks, and clearly one of the risks of being networked and always on is not being able to switch off.

The risk of burnout…
    Burnout doesn't discriminate by age: recently I was working with a manager in her late twenties, coaching her through a time of change. As we talked it became clear she had suffered burnout, and although her commitment to her employer and the work they did remained strong, the pressure to take on more work and work longer and longer hours had simply led her to a point of complete exhaustion and a fair degree of cynicism. The pressure came from those around her and from those above: the company, a well known Silicon Valley start up experiencing massive and rapid growth, offered all sorts of exciting opportunities for career growth. Whose fault was the burnout? The company's, or the individual's, or both? The answer is complex: we can see that the circumstances leading to burnout were a blend of culture (internal /organizational and external /the industry), as well as the result of organizational pressure and individual choices. Fortunately as part of her recovery the manager in question was able to negotiate a three month period of unpaid leave, though even that itself prompted a fair degree of soul-searching as they worked through the career implications of being absent from the workplace for three months.

Digital Discipline

Earlier we mentioned the risk of becoming enslaved to our device/s… It turns out that our dependency could be as much physiological as emotional/behavioral. The quick high, a measurable dopamine hit to the amygdale we get when we respond to the 'ping' of our device, whether it's to swipe a notification or make a selection, is completely addictive.

The need to be needed is inescapable for most people. In the workplace, especially one where staff are working remotely and unseen, the need for appreciation, for affirmation, in other words the need to be needed and to receive feedback is primal and unavoidable.

Habits—whether good or bad, helpful or dangerous—tend to form quickly.

We've all seen it, and many of us are guilty of having done it: surreptitiously sliding a phone out of a pocket or into view and checking for a notification. For the most part this is a conditioned or learned response. I remember the first time I was having a detailed planning conversation with a colleague in mid-town Manhattan and suddenly, without warning they pulled their phone out, quickly looked at it, tapped a few times and then put it back in their pocket. I was astonished: what was so urgent that it had to be dealt with that moment? I said nothing… and tried to get back into the flow. A few moments later, it happened again. With my colleague momentarily lost in the blue glow, I peered over to see what had taken their attention. It was a listserv email, and the phone had simply buzzed once as it received a push email. It was deleted and my colleague looked up again. At that moment we realized that the habit had become an addiction. It was unconscious: and awful. What had we become?

As almost all who have a smart phone will attest: staying the right side of polite and avoiding being distracted requires masterful self-discipline. Yet we have to learn how to regain control. And rebuild trust and respect. In our organizations as much as in our lives outside of work, we have become addicted to our devices.

Default Notification Settings

One of the challenges identified by those we spoke to in the course of researching this book is the tyranny of our default notification settings. Without a proactive approach, we are subject to the notifications and noises determined by the software developers. And it's not always clear whether they have our best interests at heart! If ever you've tried setting up a smartphone, you will realize that you have an incredible array of options, and each app can be configured entirely to your preference, assuming you have both the patience and the understanding of the various cryptic instructions before you. In simple terms, carefully changing the notification settings will go a long way towards re-balancing the overload. Why don't we do it?

We have created the 'instant response' culture by rewarding the reactive approach. Speed has become the dominant factor in measuring success. Taking time to think is seen as a weakness. Everything has to be done at breakneck speed. Leaders send emails at the weekend and expect an immediate reply. They may not say this explicitly, but their behavior gives them away. People who respond over the weekend will end up in an email conversation that has moved the subject on substantially by Monday morning. Without intervention by leaders, we accelerate towards a fast moving series of communications where quality of decisions gives way to speed and quality of life gives way to stressful working patterns.

The 24/7 nature of instant electronic communications is both a blessing and a curse. It gives us freedom to communicate at times to suit ourselves. It allows us to manage our own time effectively by giving us a choice about where to do our 'desk' work. But it also allows others to interrupt our personal time and pressurize us to respond when we should be relaxing. It encourages Productivity gurus tell us to switch off our notifications if we need to concentrate and be productive. They have good reason to do so. Without our intervention and instruction, our devices will rule us, clamoring for our attention.

With more and more devices in the workplace the potential for distraction is endless. Short attention spans, regular interruptions, frequent distractions, even the best noise-cancelling headphones, are no guarantee of being uninterrupted. Factor in open plan layouts or screens between cubicle and the ability to concentrate becomes elusive indeed. With culture being, in essence, the way we do things around here, we see and experience the all pervasive impact of technology, for better and also for worse, and many would say we have reached a point of digital overload. To coin a popular slogan, 'How can we take back control? How can we change this culture we have unwittingly created?'

Key Learnings for Leaders

Where previous technology made things easier and faster, digital technology has yet to show it is making life easier. Faster yes, but the sheer amount is causing severe overload.

The flexibility that 'always on' mobile technology offers is welcomed, but allowing it to stretch the working day unreasonably will result in a toxic environment.

Leaders whose communication to employees extends to long hours and weekends are, by their example, saying 'this is what it takes to get on here'.

Organizations that continue with 'command and control', hierarchical cultures are operating in a way that is totally at odds with today's workforce expectations and this is exacerbated by digital technology.

The ever increasing amount of information coming from a plethora of platforms, with email typically the biggest culprit, is placing employees under an enormous and consistent pressure.

Leaders who believe multi-tasking is boosting their employees' productivity are confounded by the weight of evidence against this.

Our addiction to mobile devices is exacerbated by our need to be needed and to please those who contact us by an immediate response. Leaders should adopt a more logical, sensible approach as an example to be followed.

5

The Challenge of Technology

Cliff Dennett and Mike Johnson

Connected digital technologies have brought some amazing tools and information resources to leaders. We have data and analytic capability that would amaze Henry Ford, leading to incredible advances in efficiencies and interconnectedness through supply chains. At the same time, over the past four decades, leaders have become soaked with information and opinion. The fears of missing out and of being wrong are contributing to significantly increased stress levels and lack of creativity in our companies. The 'smart' phone has become the digital overlord of digital overload. Being always on feels tiring and we have not recognized enough the impact on wellbeing that connecting digital technologies have had. Commercially-driven algorithms are dominating the choices about which information each of us receives, resulting in the reinforcement of dominant logic, arguably to the detriment of critical thinking.

C. Dennett (✉)
FutureWork Forum, Birmingham, UK
e-mail: cdennett@mac.com

M. Johnson
FutureWork Forum, Lymington, UK
e-mail: mike.ajohnson@michaeljohnsonassociates.co.uk

© The Author(s) 2018
P. Thomson et al. (eds.), *Conquering Digital Overload,*
https://doi.org/10.1007/978-3-319-63799-0_5

Have you thought that for most of us, one of the least-used apps on our smartphones is the phone! I'm not even sure why we call them phones anymore.

Technology has changed the way we work and has also changed the way we feel about work. This has happened over an incredibly accelerated period and probably during most of your personal working lives.

The history of digital computing is well documented and described in many different ways. I try here to provide a brief history, summarizing some of the complex impacts on leadership as a discipline.

Digital technology growth can be broken down into six epochs, or shifts. Each grew out of its predecessor and each caused a seismic change in worker activity, with hindsight probably requiring a significant leadership response that in HR terms has been perhaps largely lacking. As technology and world trading dynamics grew in complexity, organizations began outsourcing their IT to specialist companies. As this technology became evermore integrated into the businesses' core operations, business process outsourcing became the mantra. Large companies paid other large companies huge sums of money to redesign their core business operations around the opportunities that global connectivity brought. Then mobile arrived and everything changed again. It's undeniable that IT has brought massive efficiencies to company operations but at what cost to the wellbeing of employees.

The Six Quantum Shifts of technology can be summarized as:

1. The emergence of digital data storage, processing and analysis
2. Local and wide area networks provide physical connections between digital machines
3. The World Wide Web, providing a far simpler way for non-techies to access information
4. Growing now: The Algorithmic Web, The Internet Of Interruption
5. **Emerging** now: The Internet of Things
6. Near future: The Networked Human Gadget

Each change between shifts has been a quantum leap in information activity. In fact, the whole journey could be summarised as: information, interconnection, interruption, integration. At each stage a set of new, unprecedented network connections happens, often within a few years, that fundamentally changes our relationship with technology and latterly, with each other. Here's a summary of each one, with a focus on shift 4 (our current epoch):

Shift 1 (1970s, standalone computing) brought new sources of data and analytical capacity to leaders. Judgements became based more on data and statistical prediction, that supplemented the gut-feel and experienced-based decision-making of the past. Leaders gained more access to internal performance data that assisted decision-making, results orientation and process automation. Leadership arguably shifted focus towards trying to extrapolate from the past and predict the future through the analysis of data. Drawing from scientific disciplines, the reinforcement of opinion through a significantly higher level of data analysis added credibility to decision-making.

Shift 2 (1980s, LANs and WANs create connected computing) brought a veritable ocean of new information and along with it, significantly enhanced data analysis capability for leaders, resulting in a focus on data-informed decision-making, connected supply chains and the birth of true web-based views of the world. New data analysis requirements blossomed, with IT becoming, for the first time, a dominant new strategic function. Word processing, spread-sheeting and the birth around 1987 of the soon-to-be ubiquitous Powerpoint and Excel, brought IT tools out of IT data centers and onto the desks of millions of managers in functional departments. Forward-thinking Leaders integrated external supply chains and created efficiencies across internal departments.

Shift 3 (1990s, the World Wide Web) connected a firehose to that ocean, blasting an incessant and often unfathomable stream of data at leaders (driven largely by email and other information systems). For business leaders and organizational innovators, it was a no holds barred race to find the best data and the best data analysts. The outside world started pouring data inside organisations and new analytical frameworks emerged to try and sense-make. Over a couple of decades, information became democratized, while the rise of search engines and ultimately the ubiquitous Google, led to incredible access to just-in-time information and connectivity anytime, anywhere. From this point on, leaders had 24/7 access to market information from the Web and workers started to become socialized to gathering information and learning online themselves.

Shift 4 (our current epoch from mid 2000s, the Age of Interruption) brought mobile devices, social networks and emerging AI and 'bot' technology. The information flows, once kept largely within data centers, then pouring onto workers' desktops now stretched out into the pockets, the coffee and bedside tables and the restaurant dinner tables of those same workers. The 'always on' firehose kept delivering, unstoppable, even when leaders left the office, leading directly to an Internet of Interruption and with it that feeling of having to be 'always-on.' The mobile phone plus social media, added to the always-ubiquitous email, conspire to become the digital overlord of digital overload. We even created a name for it; 'Nomophobia' the fear of not having access to your mobile, in turn instilling the dreaded 'FOMO'; Fear Of Missing Out. Don't think you suffer from this? Put your phone in flight mode for a day (or leave it at home) and see how often you pine for its dulcet pings and naughty vibrations.

For the 200,000 years or so of human existence (depending of course on your position on the creationist—scientist scale!), if a tiger was charging towards you, it really was charging towards you, instigating the fight or flight mode. It's only been in the last hundred years or so that we've been able to create moving imagery and bring it into the TVs of the world, whereby a tiger can be seeming to run towards you, but it's not a real one. Our biological systems haven't caught up with this yet (technology is too early in our evolutionary response cycle) so we flinch, or duck behind a settee, or jump, scream or dig an elbow into your partner.

I think a similar thing has happened with connecting digital technologies. Whatever it is in our psyche that creates FOMO, which must be some kind of evolutionary response that has helped us stay alive, hasn't adapted to digital tech (presumably it's some kind of evolutionary way of us developing more intelligence and therefore becoming stronger than the other tribes). I guess, it may well take a few generations before we stop jumping out of our seats for a horror movie let alone before we stop checking our emails.

One mobile telephone operator recently told me that they collect two billion data events (locations, app uses, messaging etc.) *every day* from phone users in the UK alone. All those pings, vibrations, dings, and notifications cry for your increasingly time-poor, limited attention. Little surprise then that Leaders began to feel overwhelmed and demands on time and attention seemed to escalate dramatically. With social media came algorithms, (created largely out of the advertising-driven business models of social media) to try and keep the firehose filled with information that is most likely to resonate with you as an individual (reasons laid at the door of Trump-mania and the bafflement of Brexit). This coincided with the exponential rise in stress and a subsequent decrease in creativity in established organizations that often doesn't sit well with the need for solving complex problems. At this stage our hard-pressed, often confused business leaders became concerned about their always-on workers' ability to remain task-focused and confusion arose about role definitions. Significant blurring (the grey work space) arose between work and home life and a rise in superficiality, fake news and 'alternative facts' dominated newspaper headlines making deciding between fact and fiction increasingly difficult.

The technology trundles on trying to correct its weaknesses through ever-more intelligent self-learning algorithms and auto-fact checking to try and decrease the fake news. The problem these advances don't solve though is dealing with the firehose. It's all very well if the fact-checkers clear the murkiness from the water and the algorithms make sure the water is at exactly your ideal temperature, but it's still blasting at you, whether clear or not. It's still a firehose and it's getting stronger. If you were a laptop absorbing the information your eyes are bombarded with, you'd crash within a week. Many employees do. Roll on that weekend and 2-4-1 cocktails on a Friday night!

We all seem busier than ever with the world's information (if Google's indexed it) literally at our fingertips but I'm not sure the firehose has made us any more wise than our predecessors. Being able to ask the internet anything, anytime is a truly amazing convenience. When we control it; when we use it for questions which we have ourselves formulated, we have an incredible resource. But we have to recognize that often we do not feel in control and are not proactively searching to develop wisdom for our own questions. For much of the time we are being reactive, trying to resist the firehose with the mental equivalent of a tennis racquet. Being proactive feels good, like you're in control, moving forward, progressing. Being reactive feels bad, like you have no control, not moving anyway (or being pushed everywhere).

We have traded the:

- richness of face-to-face communication for the paucity of email
- depth of debate for the shallowness of the headline
- search for wisdom for the immediacy of fake news

If knowledge is knowing a tomato is a fruit, and wisdom is knowing not to put one in a fruit salad, then we're currently all fruit and no salad! By the way, when I searched the web for who said this about knowledge, wisdom and tomatoes, Google pointed me to Wikipedia who reports that Miles Kington said this first, so I'll go with that. But did he? How would we know? Where's your nearest library to validate this? Do you care? Have you started Googling this yet? If you have, wait 10 minutes, now check your Facebook: any ads for Miles Kington books appearing yet? Got a deal yet from Amazon on the 'Bumper Book Of Franglais'?

Developing at the same time as this 'corporate IT' is the world of 'entertainment IT' and most notably, computer gaming. From the humble 'tennis' game of Pong right through to today's ultra-realistic, fully immersive multi-dimensional experiences, gaming has brought a level of engagement still not found in corporate IT, but it's coming.

Despite the entertaining and often seemingly trivial nature of computer games, its industry revenues eclipse that of the film industry. In the same way that mobile devices brought corporate IT into the pockets of managers, so did they also bring gaming to the masses. Up until the development of the smartphone, computer gaming was largely the domain of (mostly male) teenagers, operating complex and expensive gaming consoles from their bedrooms. The combination of smartphones and social gaming[1] smashed the doors open to gamers of all ages, genders and professions. Within just a few years, the most common demographic for a game player was 30+ females with a college education and a professional job. Mums had invaded the territories of their spotty teenage sons.

Games are just another IT system, built for users to achieve specific goals, quite often, using the IT system collaboratively. For many years now, millions of people who have never met, come together to team up, adopt specific roles and immerse themselves in a world to destroy dragons, or beat an enemy army. These online games require quick wits, cooperation with people you've never met and strategic thinking. Think about that yourself for a second: that's millions of people, collaborating in complex project teams, with people they have never met, from countries all around the world, in real time to solve tactical and strategic problems. Hasn't that been the dream of HR organizations all around the world?

These things are easily dismissed as pure entertainment and therefore not relevant to organizations but the main job of the game designer is to make their IT service so addictive to use that you can't wait to get back to it. Corporate IT to date has been focused around efficiencies and cost savings but now newer applications have realized the benefits of great user interface design and are taking inspiration from games and apps to build much more user-friendly corporate IT. Gaming approaches are finding their way into the designs of organizational IT systems, so if you think you're hooked on email now, wait until the video game companies get hold of you!

Shift 5 (IoT: Internet of Things) will dramatically increase the capacity and content of the firehose as more and more 'things' send information to each other without cessation. The interruptions will become worse and the systems of the world will become ever more transparent. Public and private sector leaders will find themselves diving deeper into bottomless seas of information. As things (cars, homes, traffic lights, roads networks, public transport, white goods etc.) become hackable, cybersecurity will become more dominant in the headlines.

The physical boundaries between the home, workplace and public spaces will continue to blur, requiring a new mindset from our leaders. VR (virtual reality) will significantly impact healthcare and education. Robotics will help keep our cities clean and safer. Intelligent mobility systems will render private vehicle ownership a thing of the past, moving people around in a seamless multi-modal fashion. Local additive manufacturing (3D printing) will alleviate freight transport congestion and logistics integration will result in ever closer integration between supply chains. Leadership will become even more about information curation, critical thinking and gelling teams around common purpose.

Shift 6 (The arrival of the Human Gadget) connects the human (us) to the network, breaking through the skin/chip barrier, bypassing the sluggishness of our own capacity/ability (mostly typing and speech) and thereby connecting the high-bandwidth, high-speed processing capacity of our minds together. This will render existing interfaces (keyboards and touchscreens) obsolete, as messaging from our minds flood into our global physical networks. As this final 'speed bump' in our headlong drive forwards is removed, the amount of information being exchanged globally will escalate dramatically and new protocols to police attention and interruption will be needed. Digital health will drive the change as national health services seek dramatically different ways to save money and increase service. Leaders may have access to real-time stress profiles (and a rise in employee lawyer-bots to micro-sue for damages) of their people and perhaps employees will become highly *monitorable* and consequently more *monetizable*, in the same way that the decades of the 1980s and 1990s IT revolutionized the way production lines were managed. Organizational boundaries and legal forms are likely to look significantly different as blockchain activity impacts across society. Leadership as a skill and activity may become devolved to 'the network' where everyone receives virtual, distributed coaching. More on this later.

So this is the technological landscape that we leaders are moving through, perhaps a landscape that feels increasingly alien, the more we connect to it. 'Don't be so binary!' is the call from people looking for more ambiguity, more creativity, more critical thinking, yet when our dominant systems are built on 1s and 0s, this becomes increasingly harder. It will continue to become harder unless we leaders give the problem some focus.

Technology and Leadership

A 2015 McKinsey report[42] suggested that four kinds of behaviors account for 89% of leadership effectiveness; Being supportive, results oriented, seeking different perspectives and solving problems effectively. Trying to support others too much via email is largely accepted as ineffective and technology has certainly brought us a myriad of ways to collect data and monitor results. However, it is technology's impact on the latter two (seeking different perspectives and problem solving) that is most troubling and probably contributing to higher stress levels and depression among an increasingly roster of shorter-than-ever term CEOs.

Technology's Impact on Seeking Different Perspectives

In July 2016, the UK voted to leave the European Union. For many people, the public debate (such that there was one) that preceded the national referendum, was played out within the 'walled gardens' of the social media giants, Facebook and Twitter. Within these global, opinion-rich networks, complex algorithms determined which of the 31m UK Facebook users received which bite-sized headline and when. Like the binary basis upon which all our digital lives are based, the referendum outcome could only be one of two things; yes or no, on or off, one or zero. The UK ended up with zero (or one, depending on your perspective!).

The deep complexity, history and implications contained in this deceptively simple in-or-out question were almost unfathomable; far beyond the comprehension of most of a busy population. Whether university-educated, brought up in the 'school of life', from the north, south, rich or poor, politician, pole-dancer, policeman or postman, some questions are just too complex to be answered and certainly too complex to be answered when trying to hold down a full-time job and within a few short months of an in or out binary campaign.

Of course, some people did make significant efforts to understand the intricacies of the debate, and intricate they were; the subtleties of global trade deals, the intertwined nature of UK and EU law, the impact of (im)migration, differences between the EU, Europe, EURO, the single market, common market, customs union and the free trade area. What the deal was with Iceland, Norway and Switzerland? What is Article 50 and The Great Repeal Bill? If the UK leaves, can the British still holiday in Spain, should they invest in Euros, will French colleagues still be able to work in the UK? Will our bananas bend more?

Digging deeper encourages debate; the more you find out, the more you want to discuss and create greater clarity. Like a rising tide, healthy debate encourages all ships to rise, everyone becomes richer as a result of the discourse. As Joseph Jubert, the 18th century French philosopher, remarked 'The aim of argument, or of discussion, should not be victory, but progress.' In this massively connected world, where thick fiber-optic cables and strong wireless LAN networks join the world's tribes like never before, what happened within these walled gardens of binary ones and zeroes? Did Jubert's discussions take place and did they result in progress for those involved?

The software code that powers the interruptive nature of social media is designed ultimately to achieve one overarching commercial goal; sell more advertising. Facebook's software for determining what content you see in your newsfeed can apparently take into account over 100,000 different factors. The more relevant the content is to you, the more you will engage with the platform and the more data about you Facebook can collect and sell to brands in the form of advertising effectiveness.

As people chose their side in the Brexit debate, social media's algorithms rapidly responded. The more you liked, commented on, shared and published content that supported your existing worldview, the more the algorithms responded by narrowing down the content shown, to fit within that world view. It all happens in a matter of a few posts; your dominant logic is reinforced, competing ideas are consigned to the back-burner and the validity of your own original choices are constantly reinforced by the platform.

More reflective thinkers, who like to give time for wider research, who enjoy holding in mind competing thoughts and who dive deep into complex problems remain largely immune from this algorithmic impact. They have the desire and can allocate their time to looking beyond the algorithm, in the same way as some people would get their news from a variety of papers, or watch news channels with competing political ambitions. For an increasing percentage of the population (continuously 'soaked' by that fire hose of data), such expansive thought is a luxury and it is far easier to sit back, click a mouse, share a meme and absorb the barrage of byte-sized click-bait headlines, tailored to your existing world view.

Social media is going corporate. For years, internal corporate IT systems have sought to provide employees with context-specific, timely answers to questions such as; Have we done 'X' before? Who do we have with expertise in 'Y'? Which templates do we have for project 'Z'? The same approaches to the algorithms of citizen social media are finding their way into the information systems of corporations, ultimately resulting in binary decision making, conflict and the tyranny (or 'wisdom'?) of crowds.

Furthermore, employees use IT systems in surprising ways that may not have the intended outcomes. Sitting in a typical high-tech London office about ten years ago, an excellent operational manager (we'll call her Trish) was responding to the latest in a line of email edicts from head office. The company (a significant IT services business with over 120,000 employees globally) was implementing a new management information system to collate employee skills. The idea was that if the company could capture the vast array of qualifications, skills and experience of its workforce in one massive database, then that database could be searched by anyone looking for a particular skill-set. Seemed very logical at the time.

As Trish started working her way through the various drop down menus, she became increasingly frustrated. None of the drop-down menu choices appeared to have an exact description of her degrees and skills and as such Trish was forced into selecting things that 'most closely' fitted with her previous experience. It was made mandatory that all employees complete their details. A share of the annual bonus would depend on it.

Trish left and came back to the system a number of times, mostly leaving it in a state of despair. After all, who wants to dilute their own skills history into an inexact database, used by an employer. In one session, after about twenty minutes of trying to best portray her background using the options available, she began almost randomly selecting traits and skills just to get through the mandatory process. At one point, Trish selected Japanese as a language skill, even though she couldn't speak a word. Trish always fancied going to Japan and reasoned that if the company was daft enough to enforce such a system on its intelligent workforce, maybe they'd be daft enough to automatically send her to Japan someday.

I never did find out if Trish made it to Japan but the company did achieve its goal of 100% compliance. It may have believed it now had a system that had captured the rich background of all 120k+ employees globally. HR managers would have perhaps drawn satisfaction from the 'successful' implementation of the company-wide system and there was probably a big tick-in-the-box for a job well done at management meetings. All of this though, at what cost to the productivity and motivation of the workforce and for future strategic decision-making.

Technology's Impact on Effective Problem Solving

A common tactic used by riot police to control crowds is to blast them with a high-pressure water jet. The incessant 'noise' of the Internet often feels like this with leaders and workers constantly fighting against the blast of interruptions in their quest to just get things done. There are two reasons why leaders should be concerned about protecting their people from the relentless and deafening onslaught of noise.

The first is noise's detrimental impact on creativity. A 2014 report by Forrester and Adobe,[43] suggests that companies who actively foster creativity can demonstrate higher revenue growth than those who don't and creativity is a key ingredient of effective problem-solving. Intuitively, the world appears to be getting more complex, stress levels are increasing, problems of depression, particularly among the young, are getting worse and it feels like the more you have, the harder things are. At the same time, resources for the majority of people are becoming scarcer so we are being asked to solve more complex problems with fewer resources. This poses the question: 'Does technology enhance or block the opportunity for creative thought?'

Connecting technologies such as the internet certainly connect us with far more information than ever before. People now come into contact with as much information in a single day as our grandparents would have done in a whole month. In one sense this access to information should be a goldmine of creative input; a vast well of inspiration to draw on. However, it is almost commonplace now to try and test your own solution against the opinion of the masses. If I arrive at some apparently original solution to a complex work-based problem, before I bring that to my supervisor, surely I should do my 'due diligence' and check with the 'informed masses' online. The problem is, there will always be problems, Google will always find millions of search results, the confusing array of pros and cons for your previously original (and now seemingly commonplace) solution will confuse and dilute the original spark of genius. The internet just rained on your parade before it even left the depot for people to see it; your innovation is old hat and by the way, it doesn't work!

As well as being an incredible global resource of information, the internet can be a highly effective destroyer of dreams. The beginning of an online search can feel like a dive into adventure but can rapidly immerse you in world of naysayers and 'been-there-before'rs'. A set of hard facts on search page one are disputed on search page two. This constant barrage of conflicting evidence, competing opinion and war stories from those who've been there before can suffocate a new idea past its first breath. As fast as your beautiful organic mind creates seedlings of ideas, the digital internet stamps all over them before they see their first burst of sunlight. As the humorist, H.L. Mencken, once remarked 'there is always a well-known solution to every human problem: neat, plausible, and wrong'.

It's easy to see how the confidence for independent decision-making and taking a risk can be squashed. If you're trying to think outside the box, perhaps the internet isn't the best place because there are no walls to that box, no way to get outside of it. The box is already too big to see the size and a host of exponential factors like Moores Law ensure that the box is already so big, it might as well not be a box at all.

In one sense, this is why it's so important to leap out of the 1s and 0s of an online world that is so set up to quash your ideas. Anyone who has ever tried to create a brand through committee knows what the end result is. It becomes at best, the mean of everyone else's thinking; an average in a world of me-toos. Think of the motivational results of this. Everyone on the team comes armed with creative input from their own rich perspectives and the end result, whether it takes an hour or a month, is a diluted mix of everyone's thoughts. To corrupt an old advertising adage: 'A thought for everyone is a thought for no one'. People join with high expectations, their ideas gradually smashed with the hammer of crowd-based logic to leave us all feeling completely deflated and decidedly underwhelmed.

This is the tyranny of crowdsourcing, a recent online 'buzz-movement'. Using crowds as a strategy to arrive at solutions devalues context-based individual human thought. It arrives at 'mind-memes' where the collective mind of a team, organization or online community is harnessed to output an average of everyone's opinions. This is comfortably risk averse (the modern-day 'no one got fired for buying from IBM' adage) but not necessarily appropriate for a fast-paced, changing, ever more complicated world.

The second reason we should be concerned about shielding our people from the noise has to do with flow and productivity. The paradox of our time is that creativity is needed to solve evermore complex problems and the technology most of us use to help in that problem-solving is highly interruptive in nature such that states of 'flow' are hardly ever reached, let alone maintained.

Technology's Impact on Engagement

Part of the reason for the apparent disconnectedness in the workplace, the feeling of alienation among workers, the stress felt by leaders has to do with technology's illusion of efficiency. The assumption is that; looking at organizations through the cells of a spreadsheet helps us understand human nature more; that keeping your phone next to you in meetings means you can remain more in touch with the organization; that the Tweeting during a speech at a public conference helps engage a wider audience; that sharing pictures of your dinner in a restaurant helps your friends relate to your happiness and the restaurant generate more sales.

When we meet together and actively engage in dialogue we can create amazing leaps forward. If we act respectfully, be emotionally intelligent and challenge others in the name of overall progress, a small group of people can achieve incredible things. These leaps forward, the creative problem solving, the moving forward together, on the same page, are really tricky when you've all brought a window into millions of distractions into the meeting and have that window laid plainly on the table in front of you. When was the last time you were in a meeting, discussing something strategic and a phone buzzed and most of the room immediately grabbed their 'windows to the world' to see if it was something for them? Probably whenever the last meeting was you went to, that's when.

When did it become OK to bring someone into an important meeting who doesn't work for the company, who knows nothing about what you are discussing, who doesn't care anyway and who doesn't have the social skills to know when or when not to speak? Never, that's when. At some point in the last decade, the smartphone became that person. Even worse, the smartphone could be a thousand different people with a million different interruptions. Next time you have an important strategy meeting, ask your colleagues if it's OK if your wife, best mate, random stranger, journalist you've never met, or political activist comes along, just in case they have something completely unconnected, random and probably extreme to say. See how that goes down for your promotion prospects. That's your smartphone.

Our social lives are certainly not immune from these interruptions of course. This isn't just a work-based, corporate challenge. Ever since the birth of Apple's online music marketplace iTunes, the smartphone has helped people listen to their favorite music anywhere and at any time they like. But as a musician, you have a problem. You can't make much money from recorded music anymore because people are either downloading your music for free from illegal websites, watching it on YouTube for which you will receive a pittance in ad share revenue or streaming it from Spotify et al. and again, you're receiving a pittance in revenue share. The main way musicians make money from music is through live performance and associated merchandise sales; I watch Ed Sheeran at the O2 Arena and buy a £20 t-shirt while I'm there. It's big money for all concerned (including you).

This is a fine model. There really is nothing like the experience of tens of thousands of fans all enjoying an amazing live performance by a really talented artist with all of the amazing production that's possible nowadays; the lights, the lasers, the sets, the performance, incredible! Music productions are amazing shows nowadays with months of effort and hundreds of thousands of pounds of investment in creating the most amazing spectacle possible. The bands love it. Many musicians say how they live for live performance. The fans love it. Nothing like being part of a legendary one-off performance, the 'I was there' moment. The business loves it. Record labels, festival organizers, music promoters, publishers, merchandisers, venues, bars, take-aways all do very well out of it. It doesn't matter whether your thing is rock, pop, opera or jazz, the experience of a well produced live music performance can form some of your most engaging and lasting memories.

Well, they do, but only if the audience is having a good time. That little smartphone is making the good time, a little less good and a bit more mediocre.

Think about it. You go to a concert. Whether you are jumping up and down in a mosh pit at a heavy metal concert, or sedately seated in an operatic recital and you, along with most of the fifty thousand people there, are watching this carefully curated, finely produced grand spectacle of musical accomplishment and theatrical production through a tiny 3inch by 5inch screen, held in a wobbly hand, recording audio in the lowest quality form. You've paid £50 to go and record a performance on a £500 device which you will never watch, completely missing the atmosphere of the live performance, which all those hundreds of thousands of pounds have been spent creating.

The band on the stage is losing interest because you can't really clap in case you drop the £500 device in your hands and in any case, you're too busy not watching them through the screen you're holding in the air, obscuring the view of those behind you.

It's an odd situation where we feel compelled to record high fidelity real life on a pretty low fidelity virtual format, missing the real in the vanity of saving the inferior virtual version.

Life in organizations can feel a bit like this; with all our analysis and spreadsheets and emails and chat channels and social media groups, working in companies is starting to feel like being at a rock concert and completely missing the gig.

What Happens When You Become the Gadget: Interruptions at Biological Scale

For many people who aren't regularly thinking about the impact of technology on our lives, words like robot, cyborg or android can summon up dark visions of machines taking over the world, of the dominance of technology over man and often of the impending destruction of humankind against the rise of the machine. Even in less cataclysmic predictions, technology will apparently still render the human form largely useless in the workplace, apart from perhaps the most creative or technical jobs. That seminal management thinker, Warren Bennis once remarked that 'The factory of the future will have only two employees, a man and a dog. The man will be there to feed the dog. The dog will be there to keep the man from touching the equipment.'

The power of our individual brains is self-evident yet researchers continue to struggle to define exactly how powerful. Usually comparative research attempts to draw conclusions by comparing the processing speed of the brain with the latest generation of CPUs and estimates vary widely from 'about the same' to an estimate of in the range of one thousand to one million times faster than the latest computer processors. Whatever the comparative speed, it is largely our output mechanisms that make us slower than computers when interfacing with the outside world.

Let's try this. Look up from this book for a second and imagine how much visual information your eyes are currently taking in and the 'streaming' to the image processing areas of your brain. Mary Potter and her brain and cognitive sciences team at MIT recently estimated[44] that the human brain can process entire images that the eye sees for as little as 13 milliseconds. Computers still struggle with facial recognition, whereas we can easily recognize even an aged face. Then think about the speed on the output side. How long would it take you to describe verbally, or type out in an email, a decent, rich description of the scene you last looked at?

In truth, we really only have two modes of output; speech and physical movement of our limbs. The fastest form of the latter being our ability to type (and now swipe, touch etc.) using our touch-screen mobile devices. The disparity between input and processing speed and then our ability to output information is vast. Other studies suggest that information is moved around the brain at about the same speed as the average Ethernet, somewhere around 10–50 megabits per second. So, we can take in vast amounts of information, process and turn this information into vast stream of complex thought almost in an instant, yet to output this in any rich, meaningful context can take minutes, hours, possibly even days.

In his widely viewed 2006 TED talk on creativity in education[45] (45m+ views at time of writing), educator and creativity commentator, Ken Robinson half-jokingly talked about how professors 'look upon their body as a form of transport for their heads'. The thought of our brains and other organs being 'hard-wired' through some intrusive biological connection to an outside computer scares many people. It feels like the last protection for our humanity is the physical barrier of our own skins. Even if we lose control of the outside world, as long as we keep technology out of our bodies, maybe we can still hold onto some form of internal control, of remaining human.

Yet we have been absorbing technology into our bodies for years and have been gradually networking ourselves to the outside world. For many of us, spectacles provide a welcome upgrade to underperforming eyes, helping us maximize those high-capacity input channels to our brains. Some use external attachments to optimize the aural inputs entering our thoughts via our ears. Millions of people around the world benefit from implanted pacemakers that regulate their heartbeat. Today's wearable devices like Apple Watch and Fitbit can already monitor and transmit remotely heart rate, physical activity, sleeping patterns and blood pressure.

Currently the physical barrier between our minds and the internet prevents us from interfacing with all this information at maximum speed. It's our fingers that usually slow us down. Highly equipped for a history of physical tool-making, our ten digits would not be the optimum configuration should an engineer be asked to design an output interface between man and computer. Digital health will be the driving force for ever-deeper integration of our human selves with the digital network.

Interruptions at Biological Scale

For a technology that has existed for less than 30 years and for which its major social applications have only been interrupting us for the past decade or so, the Internet seems completely entwined in our lives.

Now the technology is interruptive and instant. In exchange for gaining free access to 'friend' updates and platforms of exchange we must accept both the intrusiveness of advertising (it's become so pervasive that marketers have changed the vocabulary to hide it to 'sponsored stories') and the algorithmic selection of the 'information' that is delivered to us. We are also in danger of losing the meaning in what we do. Information used to be power but when we can all access that information, who holds the power? It seems currently that the power sits in the code that makes up the algorithms that's causing those interruptions.

What happens when the interruptions happen at individual biological or even cognitive scale; when you become the gadget? Currently my attention is constantly distracted by the 'ping' of the notification. Soon even your thoughts and possibly your dreams become the playground of the advertiser as computer science researchers combine forces with biologists and engineers to dramatically improve the man-machine interface, currently restricted through our hands. If you think you are sometimes paralyzed by information overload, how will we lead in a world where thoughts are connected? What happens to trust? How much do we really want to know about the true thoughts of our employees?

This fire hose, drenching the user in the floodtide and spray of information, is not going to dry up. Even in the most bleak sci-fi dystopian thriller (read no doubt on an e-book) there's no way to turn it off. Somewhere along the last 30 years we lost the key, now it's snapped off in the lock. Whether or not we drown in data remains to be seen.

Key Learnings for Leaders

Key skills for succeeding in a modern age; creativity, problem-solving and engagement, appear to have been negatively impacted, as we increasingly view the real world through the cells of a spreadsheet or the screens of a smartphone.

As technology penetrates our world through Internet Of Things sensors and then through our protective skin layer, tapping into the electrical signals that power our thoughts, these interruptions will become significantly worse, unless we proactively develop strategies to deal with them.

With social media came algorithms, to try and keep the firehose filled with information. This has coincided with an exponential rise in stress and a subsequent decrease in creativity in established organizations that often reduces capacity to solve complex problems.

Technology has affected four leadership behaviors made up of being supportive, results oriented, seeking different perspectives and solving problems effectively.

The same approaches to the algorithms of citizen social media are finding their way into the information systems of corporations, ultimately resulting in binary decision making, conflict and the tyranny (or 'wisdom'?) of crowds.

Practical leadership could respond better with increased focus on how to manage the digital firehose.

6

The Changing Human Experience of Work

Jim Ware and Susan Stucky

This chapter focuses on the nature of knowledge work and its increasing dependence on technology. More importantly, our experience of work is changing in several fundamental but little-understood ways. We believe an examination of how the digitization of work is broadly impacting the economy is central to the future of organizational leadership.

Overview

The basic experiences we have at work today are very different from the past, and we produce value in ways that were unimaginable just a few years ago. Trends of the last few decades have only become more intense. The work people do is increasingly knowledge-based, technology-dependent,

J. Ware (✉) · S. Stucky
FutureWork Forum, California, USA
e-mail: jim@thefutureofwork.net

S. Stucky
e-mail: susanstucky@gmail.com

© The Author(s) 2018
P. Thomson et al. (eds.), *Conquering Digital Overload*,
https://doi.org/10.1007/978-3-319-63799-0_6

collaborative, distributed, and location-independent. It is also becoming less visible and more disembodied, increasingly occurring 'in' cyberspace.

Two relatively new attitudes toward work point to a broadening spectrum of views about work. Firstly, most people, especially Millennials, now expect to be able to bring their individual and social experiences, and their learning and communication styles, to work; work is now an expression of who we are and what we care about.

Second, at the other end of the spectrum, many people are rejecting (at least partially) the work-centric lifestyle seemingly enabled by digital technologies. Pointers to this trend range from the recently resurrected calls for basic income to an outright 'refusal of work'.[46]

At the same time, digital technologies are absorbing more and more work that people used to do. In fact, the digital transformation of work now underway has evolved to such a point that society is experiencing wrenching, one might say, existential, change. Data-driven algorithms are taking over skilled work, even knowledge work, that people used to do, while machine-learning techniques are beginning to conduct knowledge work that humans can't realistically do at all.

For example, IBM's 'Watson' technology can help researchers identify novel drug targets faster by far than medical researchers can. And it recently has proven to be highly effective at enhancing the diagnosis of breast cancer in partnership with 'human' physicians.[47]

Knowledge work used to be a kind of sacred space for people. Meanwhile, highly-skilled blue collar work is disappearing, and what is left for humans to do looks suspiciously like knowledge work, requiring a kind of digital dexterity and, for now, sophisticated interpretation of digital information. For instance, underground mining is increasingly being conducted by equipment that can work to some extent autonomously. Instead of sitting in a cab on an earth-mover, human operators now sit above ground and keep an eye on the equipment, interpreting the digital information that is presented and taking action only when their judgment tells them it is called for.

The rise of new technologies and tools, it must be remembered, is not new to the human condition. Ever since the early development of tools; baskets and spears and grinding stones, which were the labour-saving tools of their time; people have been inventing and using tools and technology to get work done more easily and quickly.

According to historian Andrew Nye, adapting to technological change is predictable in its engagement with new technologies: 'each new machine, for example, the railroad, the airplane, the television, or the assembly line, passes through a characteristic cycle of public responses: celebration, adoption, naturalization, complaint, and resignation'.[48]

The appearance of this book would suggest that society is somewhere in the zone between compliant and resignation. So, while this chapter starts signs of resignation, even cynicism, it ends with a suggestion. Perhaps the 'it' isn't digital technologies and the situation we have enabled. Perhaps 'it' is the mindset, the way of looking at these digital technologies, that needs to change. We believe that a new mindset can reduce the stress we are all feeling and suggest new approaches for introducing and applying technology to the way we work.

Taking our cue from what has been learned and experienced about knowledge work over the last sixty years, we believe that hiding there in plain sight is another way of looking at what we are experiencing. We believe that understanding how knowledge work works holds the key to our collective futures.

Automation 'Versus' Augmentation

From the very beginning of digital computer technology's appearance on the scene in the 1950s and 60s, two kinds of strategies for applying digital technology to human work have been proposed. One is *automation* of work that people used to do. The other is *augmentation* or *assistance* for humans in the work they continue to do.

As it turned out, for the most part automation won. It has promised and delivered on many fronts: reliability, repeatability, consistency, standardization, precision, in less time and for less cost.

In many ways automation strategies have accomplished what two early world of work pioneers, Frederick Taylor and Henry Ford, began by standardizing work into smaller and smaller increments, simplifying tasks, and driving cost and time out of the process. For decades, first 'scientific management,' and then business process reengineering, has broken work down into ever-smaller tasks, until we get to the hyper-tasking that MIT Professor Tom Malone predicted over a decade ago.[49] In the automated world, the industrial mind-set holds sway.

Augmentation, it was argued by Douglas Englebart in the 1960s,[50] was a more interesting, and ultimately more valuable, role for digital technology. He foresaw a world in which vast social complications would arise. He argued that it was only with large-scale collaboration among organizations and people that these problems could be addressed. And, as he often said, the sooner the better.

The augmentation mindset has not yet had quite the same impact that automation has had. We believe that, for far too long, automation and augmentation have been seen as competing views, not as complementary approaches to the relationship between human-based work and technology-based work.

The Changing Nature of Work

When the term *knowledge work* was first proposed by Peter Drucker in 1959[51] it served primarily to distinguish knowledge work from manual labor. First, most knowledge work is intangible and invisible, taking place inside peoples' heads, in conversations with other people, or between them and their computers.

The economy's growing dependence on information and knowledge as the source of value has profound implications for how we form teams, collaborate, and manage both work and workers.

We bring our individual experiences, expectations, and learning and communication styles to the work we do; work has become an expression of who we are and what we care about. The 'Industrial Age' valued conformity and following the rules; today's leaders value creativity and initiative and (sometimes!) a readiness to challenge accepted ways of doing things.

In the industrial era, most organizations were seeking workers who had mastered a common core of skills and who were capable of 'tending' the machines on the assembly line; workers were essentially replaceable because each station on that assembly line required the same skills and the same behaviours no matter who the individual worker was.

But when a knowledge worker joins a team the very nature of the team changes; its capabilities, its collective mindset, even its norms and expectations. Each of us is a unique individual who brings a unique combination of experiences, knowledge, and skills to work. And that is our value to the organisation.

Yet, it is only recently that the new predominance of knowledge work has finally had an impact on the design of the workplace. It was probably always true that knowledge work required the back and forth between individual, 'heads-down' work that requires uninterrupted time for concentration and focus, and interactive, collaborative conversations of all kinds. However, those distinctions did not become obvious until private offices became less and less available as organizations discovered new, less costly ways to house their staff.

Driven by the desire for more collaboration and increased serendipity and the rise of flexible work styles (along with lower cost per square foot, let's not forget), the cube walls and partitions came down. But open space doesn't work well for the heads down/regroup pattern of knowledge work. Over the past decade workplace design has evolved towards a much richer palette of individual workstations, large and small conference rooms, break-out areas, informal lounge areas, and open, public spaces.

Work is becoming increasingly knowledge-based, technology-dependent, collaborative, distributed and location-independent. It is also becoming less visible and more disembodied, increasingly occurring 'in' cyberspace.

Understanding Knowledge-Based Work

Early in his career our co-author Jim Ware worked for a large Chicago-based textbook publishing firm. One unforgettable conversation with an editor, a brilliant, well-educated woman, convinced him just how different knowledge work is from traditional, industrial-age work. She came to him in tears one afternoon to report that she had just been docked a full week's vacation.

She was supposed to be at her desk and at work every morning at 8:30 AM; her supervisor had been tracking her arrivals and claimed that over the past twelve months she had accumulated almost 40 hours of 'tardiness' (10 minutes one day, 5 minutes another, and so on).

It apparently made no difference to her supervisor that she almost never joined the parade out the door at precisely 5 PM; in fact, she regularly worked an hour or two beyond 5 PM to meet her deadlines. And she often took work home when she did leave the office.

Docking her vacation time might have been an appropriate disciplinary action if the editor had been working on an assembly line somewhere and was being paid by the hour. But she was a former secondary school teacher with a master's degree who was being paid a decent salary to collaborate with a college professor on a secondary-school math book.

Knowledge workers are different, and they work differently from assembly line workers. If you think about it, that's obvious. But in our experience an incredible number of supposedly intelligent organizational leaders don't seem to understand just how distinctive knowledge-based work is from manual labour, retail sales, and other 'industrial' forms of work.

Knowledge is not a 'thing' that you can hold in your hand, or even describe. It doesn't have weight, or colour, or smell. There are many kinds of knowledge. There is information, or data, and 'facts' about the physical world. There is an understanding of how physical objects behave, or interact with each other; how one thing can cause another, or how one chemical interacts with another (for example, how detergent neutralizes acidic juices).

There is also knowledge about patterns in nature, or in human relationships. The sun rises and sets on a predictable cycle; summer follows spring; water freezes at zero degrees Celsius. Some so-called 'knowledge' is more tenuous; and, when it is based on opinions or beliefs that do not have any basis in reality, it can be downright dangerous.

But what makes knowledge significantly different from physical things is what you can do with it (and what you can't). For example, if I have $100 and give you half of it, you now have $50 and I have $50. But if I have a special recipe for roasting a chicken and I share it with you, now we both know how to cook a delicious meal. I haven't given up anything, but now there are two of us who have the same knowledge (in fact, I probably gained some credibility and gratitude for sharing my special recipe so willingly).

Furthermore, once information has been shared it can't be taken back. Once I've told you that recipe I can't 'untell' you.

Most Work Today is Intensely Knowledge-Based

Knowledge work is fundamentally different from manual labour in several respects. First, most of it is intangible and invisible, taking place inside workers' heads and/or their computers. There is less need for physical tools and more for information access and storage. Offices filled with workstations and communication devices require new architectural designs, new kinds of desks and work surfaces, and acoustic and lighting arrangements that differ from more traditional offices based on paper-intensive processes and activities.

More importantly, the most critical aspect of knowledge work is that it cycles back and forth between individual, 'heads-down' work that requires uninterrupted time for concentration, on the one hand, and interactive, collaborative conversations of all kinds, on the other hand.

Over the past decade workplace design has evolved from the infamous (and hugely unpopular) 'cube farms' to a much richer palette of individual workstations, large and small conference rooms, break-out areas, informal lounge areas, and open, public spaces. Complaints that the 'open office' has become too popular reflect the reality that knowledge workers need different kinds of spaces for different kinds of work, and the nature of their work changes literally from hour to hour and moment to moment.[52]

One other aspect of knowledge-based work bears mentioning. The quality of the work output is much more difficult to measure, and often impossible to see. Ideas and designs are intangible results whose quality is often highly subjective. And the value of a new product or a new software program is often not clear until months or even years after the 'work' has been completed. This aspect of knowledge work makes it even more difficult than in the past to measure the impact of the workplace on the work, and on organizational productivity.

Yet outcomes-based metrics are a critical component of raising the bar; of making the workplace's strategic value clear to senior business executives.

Knowledge Work is Technology-Dependent

No one will argue that work activity today is not deeply dependent on information technology and other kinds of technology. Recently during a temporary power outage that made Internet access virtually non-existent, one manager in a data-intensive business asked the only slightly facetious question, 'Do we even exist without power?' Uninterruptible power supplies, wireless access, all kinds of building sensors, and even digitally-based, self-enforcing lease contracts are now an essential part of any workplace designer's toolkit.

There are at least three very profound ways that our information access and personal communications have changed in the last decade because of digital technologies. Three realities that most of the world takes for granted today, but that are totally unprecedented in human history. As Jim Ware first reported in *Making Meetings Matter*:

First, with a relatively inexpensive computer and an Internet connection, **anyone can access almost any information almost anywhere in the world** – and at almost no incremental cost. Granted, digital data is only part of the information that matters. Nevertheless, you can find almost anything you want whenever you want it, with very little advance planning, somewhere online (and where it is actually located is almost completely irrelevant). Just type your question or topic into your favourite search engine, and start digging.

Second, **you can connect and converse with almost any other person**, almost anywhere in the world, again at almost zero incremental cost. And you have an incredible array of ways to connect. Landline phones still work, and email is essentially free and easy. Cell phones are everywhere (though they do have a basic fixed cost, the incremental minutes are relatively cheap). And don't forget all the other communication channels that are readily available, many of them completely free once you have online access: Skype, LinkedIn, Facebook, Twitter, Instagram, Snapchat, Tumblr, Flickr, Facetime, Pinterest, Periscope, Blab, and more.

And third, **anyone with a computer and an Internet connection can publish almost anything on a global basis.** While no one has an accurate count of how many blogs there are globally, the three major blogging platforms (Tumblr, Wordpress, and Blogger) together had over 300 million accounts at the end of 2014.[53]

And then of course there is YouTube and other video platforms. YouTube's video library grows by 100 hours every single minute of every single day – that's over 144,000 hours of new video per day! And over 6 billion hours of video are viewed every day (that's almost an hour per day for every person on earth). Yes, viewing recorded video isn't exactly a real conversation, but it certainly is an increasingly popular means of communicating ideas.

This explosive growth in the amount of information and communication being sent out and received is nothing short of staggering. There is no question we're having an unprecedented global conversation.

Admittedly, much of what has been published and uploaded to that now-ubiquitous 'Cloud' isn't the least bit interesting to many of us. But it's there to be read or viewed or listened to. And you know it's there, even if you don't attempt to access it. The two of us are convinced this explosion of choice and gigabits of accessible information is a big part of the stress and anxiety that most of us feel most of the time.

Knowledge Work is Inherently Conversational and Collaborative

Designing workplaces and work experiences that enable and encourage collaboration is *de rigueur* in 2017 and will be for many years to come.

As *Fast Company* founder Alan Webber pointed out over twenty years ago, conversation is at the very heart of knowledge-based work. Yet most of us don't recognize how dependent we are on conversations for learning, for making sense of our experiences, for building relationships, for innovation, and for sorting out how we feel about ourselves and our work.

In Webber's words:

...the revolution in information and communications technology makes knowledge the new competitive resource. But knowledge only flows through the technology; it actually resides in people – in knowledge workers and the organizations they inhabit…the manager's job is to create an environment that allows knowledge workers to learn – from their own experience, from each other, and from customers, suppliers, and business partners.

The chief management tool that makes that happen is conversation.[54]

In 2017 conversation and collaboration are central to producing economic value and to a meaningful work experience. And since work is also increasingly distributed and mobile, that means that we are deeply dependent on the technology tools that enable us to access information and engage in conversations with other people no matter where in the world that information and those people may be located.

Knowledge Work is Distributed and Flexible

You know from personal experience that many, if not most, of your work-related conversations involve communicating with people who are somewhere else.

In fact, a full *two-thirds* of knowledge work today takes place outside of corporate facilities. That sounds like a strikingly large number, but there have been numerous formal studies (some of them conducted by us[55]) clearly demonstrating that organizational work is widely dispersed across many kinds of locations (and it is rapidly becoming more so). With digital technology as a platform it doesn't matter whether the people we are interacting with are across a desk, across the room, across town, or across the ocean.

Yet one of the most common complaints we hear about letting local employees work remotely even just a day or two a week is 'How can I manage them if I can't see them?' That attitude understandably reflects many years of having immediate subordinates close by. Most managers still rely on 'management by walking around' to exercise control over their staff. The managers can see what their staff are doing, and they generally presume that their physical presence acts a constant reminder of their authority and the need for everyone to stay busy.

Again, this shift away from relying exclusively on familiar, in-person conversations among co-located individuals is yet another source of stress. Learning to work with teams that are dispersed across cities, states, and even continents requires the mastery of new skills; and, initially at least, takes more effort than walking down the hall to drop into a colleague's office for an informal chat.

Workforce flexibility and mobility, whether it is called 'telecommuting,' 'flexible work,' 'remote work,' 'distributed work,' or something else, is rapidly becoming a way of life for more and more knowledge workers. As we have noted repeatedly, technology is increasingly able to connect people with each other, with information, and with work processes no matter where on earth they happen to be.

It is a fact of life that most of the work we do and many of the conversations we experience every day are distributed. And many of those 'conversations' extend over time as well as over physical distance, adding the phenomenon of multitasking and unfinished business to the litany of consequences stemming from our growing dependence on digital tools.

Managers often worry that distributed teams suffer from a loss of the serendipity that so often leads to important business breakthroughs: those unplanned, spontaneous so-called 'corridor conversations' between people who don't interact normally while doing their jobs, or who, when they do interact, are narrowly focused on the task at hand.

But even if most people continue to prefer face-to-face meetings, the hard reality is that those meetings are becoming a smaller and smaller percentage of our work experience. We all have to learn how to work effectively with people who are in other places.

Knowledge Work is Increasingly Invisible and Disembodied

We have noted that more and more of our work activity is embedded in a wide variety of digital technologies. Another poorly-understood consequence of that digitization is that an increasing proportion of work is becoming invisible to human beings.

Once a process has been automated its 'events' and related information disappears from physical view, and it becomes visible again only when someone displays it on computer screen or, heaven forbid, prints it out on an old-fashioned sheet of paper. And that visibility is inherently partial and inscrutable, and therefore not able to be inspected or analysed. Those characteristics also make the automated process almost impervious to change and improvement.

Economist W. Brian Arthur called attention to this radical shift in the way digital work works in a 2011 *McKinsey Quarterly* article: 'Digitization is creating a second economy that's vast, automatic, and invisible'.[56]

As Arthur describes it, the automation of business processes embeds work activity that was formerly carried out by human beings into software and buries it inside a computer or another digital device. Once automated, digitized work takes place within electronic media, on servers, hard disks, and across copper wires and fibre cables.

Complex activities like financial transactions, airline flight reservations, and even formerly artisan activities like baking bread are now being carried out digitally and robotically, again requiring less space, and different kinds of space, than traditional human-based work activity.

In parallel with the other work trends described above, the continuing disembodiment of work activity creates new planning and operational challenges, and new levels of stress, for everyone in the workplace.

Knowledge Work is Difficult to Measure and Evaluate

But well before the rise of Arthur's 'second economy' most knowledge work was already taking place either inside individuals' heads or in the conversations that took place among people who were solving problems, inventing, brainstorming, and sharing ideas. Knowledge work has always been at least partially invisible and disembodied, and therefore difficult to track, measure, and evaluate.

There is a *New Yorker* cartoon that captured this challenge perfectly. It depicted a corporate office with a man leaning back in his desk chair and staring at the ceiling deep in thought, with his hands behind his neck and his feet up on the desk. Over the desk was a sign that read 'Think.' And outside his office in the hallway another man (presumably his boss) is asking a colleague, 'How do we know he's thinking about our products?'

It gets even more complicated. When the work is focused on long-term results, evaluating its quality and value is, almost by definition, highly subjective. Consider an automobile design engineer who is working on a new model that will not be completed and produced for several years. How should her supervisor evaluate her work this year and decide whether to offer her a salary increase?

Furthermore, the whole concept of productivity is an industrial-age measure of efficiency. Productivity is the ratio of output to input, typically measured in terms of the quantity of items produced in a specific time period, or with a measurable quantity of input such as person-hours or the amount of raw materials required.

Even national economic measures are typically stated in terms like output per hour, and gross domestic product, which is the total of economic value produced in a year, or a quarter. National economic growth is described as a percentage gain in the value of economic transactions.

However, with information-based activity the value is often not the *quantity* of output but its *quality*. And in many cases that quality is highly subjective; it is determined by the customer.

Here is another brief story that illustrates how knowledge work can be difficult to evaluate. In this case, a man driving a foreign sports car pulls into a service station and complains that the engine sounds horrible and is vibrating erratically. The mechanic raises the hood, listens for a moment, and goes back into the shop. He returns with a small sledge hammer and proceeds to slam it into the side of the engine as hard as he can.

The driver jumps back in horror, but the engine immediately settles down to a quiet, smooth idle. Delighted, the driver asks how much he owes for the repair. The mechanic replies '$500.'

'$500! That's outrageous! You spent less than five minutes and all you did was hit the engine!'

To which the mechanic replied, 'Okay, it's just $1 for hitting the engine, and $499 for knowing where to hit.'

Of course, in 2017 the mechanic would no doubt hook up a computer to get a reading on the engine. He would then make several subtle adjustments to the (software-based) engine control module using a sophisticated electronic tool. We suspect there are very few mechanics left today who would know 'where to hit the engine.'[57]

These examples highlight the difficulty of measuring knowledge work; assessing the value of what someone, or some group, has produced is a complex process. Often the only way to measure the value of knowledge or information is a market-based transaction in which someone pays real money to acquire the rights to an idea or other piece of intellectual property.

Yet most knowledge is produced inside organizations, insulated from the economic marketplace. Value must be judged subjectively, and thus it is frequently open to debate. And that reality is at the heart of the challenge facing all knowledge-based organizations and their leaders.

Key Learning for Leaders

Here's something we as would-be leaders need to take on board. When Knowledge Management was all the rage in the 1990s (remember them?), knowledge-based work was a central part of the conversation. Some even argued that *all* work is knowledge work since doing even simple manual labour requires at least some minimal level of human intelligence.

However, the focus of industrial-era activity was on producing physical things that can be counted and weighed, and that either do what they are designed to do, or not. And that production occurred at a measurable pace, with definable input costs. Those attributes made the calculation of productivity relatively straightforward, and it was relatively easy to calculate the amount of human labour required to produce a given quantity of output with economic value.

Today, digital technologies are impacting work activities as diverse as underground mining and medical diagnosis; and with the advance of artificial intelligence and machine learning, much more of the work being done has a strong knowledge-based component. And since virtually all of that kind of activity is digitally enabled, people are essentially tied to, and dependent on, digital screens even though they can carry out that work from almost anywhere on the planet.

Those conditions mean that just about everyone is experiencing the stresses that come from digital ubiquity, digital overload, and all the other dark features of digitalization that are being discussed throughout this book. Perhaps the most important thing for leaders to learn is to keep our minds open, shut nothing out and realize that a revolution has happened while we possibly forgot to notice how it has impacted every facet of our lives.

7

Building an Engaging Organizational Culture: A Leadership Challenge

Peter Thomson and Ben Emmens

Whereas in the past a digital strategy may have been sufficient to ensure an organization maintained its competitive advantage in a largely analog world, today, success is about being able to develop and implement strategy in a constantly changing, digital world. Successful organizations comprise people that can bridge the digital divide, navigate an ever-changing and often uncertain context, and deal with the inevitable culture shock that rapid change brings. These are the leadership behaviors that matter, and being able to use technology, rather than ending up being used by technology has to be our goal. We look at how to build organizational cultures that are engaging, and where technology is in service to organizational vision and strategy.

P. Thomson (✉)
FutureWork Forum, Henley-on-Thames, UK
e-mail: peter.thomson@me.com

B. Emmens
FutureWork Forum, London, UK
e-mail: ben@benemmens.com

© The Author(s) 2018
P. Thomson et al. (eds.), *Conquering Digital Overload*,
https://doi.org/10.1007/978-3-319-63799-0_7

89

Cultural Intelligence

Today's workplaces are characterized by multiple and often conflicting tensions. Chief of these is reconciling vision and growth (and the requisite change and adaptation) with the reality of the current state and vested interests. Any chance of success relies on a deep appreciation of culture, and in particular individual and organizational behavior. Drawing on the work of Daniel Goleman (among others), who opened our eyes to the importance of emotional intelligence, our understanding and appreciation of related concepts such as social and cultural intelligence has grown significantly over the last 10–15 years. Successful leaders, and their organizations, are the ones who have been able to navigate cultural complexity while maintaining digital fluency and relevance; this is a skill that requires deep cultural intelligence.

Cultural Intelligence (CQ) is the natural evolution from the now well-established notions of Intelligence Quotient (IQ) and Emotional Intelligence (EQ). Good leaders need all three if they are to lead effectively. CQ differs from IQ in the fact that it cannot be quantified by a score. There is no simple Cultural Intelligence scale to measure ourselves against, and indeed it is unhelpful to think of CQ as a number.

Instead we should think of Cultural Intelligence as being something which we can continuously improve and develop over the duration of our lives. We acquire it through our experiences, but also with knowledge imparted by other people whom we trust, and who trust us enough to give us their knowledge.

Developing cultural intelligence requires humility and openness: a recognition that we have a lot to learn, and a willingness to learn. For many of us, it's hard to acknowledge our addiction to technology and the problems it can create in terms of relationships and our ability to communicate, particularly listen, effectively.

When it comes to disruptive change (and digitalization is a disruptive change), leadership is the ability to hold the current state and then adaptively implement evolutionary change processes. Edgar Schein recognizes this 'the ability to perceive the limitations of one's own culture and to evolve the culture adaptively'[58] as the essence and ultimate challenge of leadership.

Building Trust

The key characteristic of an effective culture is trust. It has always been true that trust is important in building relationships and today it is critical to the success of any organization operating in a free labor market. Leaders can no longer expect blind loyalty from their workforce, they have to earn their trust. They also have to trust their workers to act responsibly when given autonomy in their working practices. Digital technology has broken down barriers and increased transparency to the stage where leaders have to show they trust their people. It is no longer sufficient to have trust on a list of corporate values without it being demonstrated through daily leadership practices.

We know from literature, research and personal experience that the level of trust in an organization has a strong link with effective co-operation and collaboration, with morale, with flexibility, with knowledge transfer and learning, with participation, with innovation, with creativity, and of course with effective leadership. We know that when trust breaks down, individuals often take fewer risks, preferring to protect themselves and play safe. Administrative controls and checking procedures tend to increase and important or sensitive information is withheld. The result is a more stressful working environment and the quality of work suffers.

It takes time to build lasting trust. It builds slowly in relationships based on experience. When leaders stick to their commitments and can be trusted by employees they will be respected and followed. When they show trust in their people by delegating responsibility and allowing them to make choices themselves they create a committed, engaged workforce. On an individual basis this relies on a personal relationship built up over the experience of working together. Building trust in a team or a whole organization is a more complex process.

In his book 'Conscious Collaboration'[59], Ben Emmens gives examples of building trust in diverse teams in the humanitarian aid sector. One involved an inter-agency working group on emergency capacity tackling the most persistent challenges in delivery of aid. With help from consultants they built a toolkit with ten criteria for trust:

Competence	—Trust based on a perception that team members are competent, and so will not let me down
Openness with information	—Trust based on the observation that other team members share information important to the team proactively and clearly
Integrity	—Trust based on the observation that other team members maintain promises, are team-oriented, and behave toward me in accordance with a moral code
Reciprocity	—Trust based on the observation that other team members are trusting and co-operative toward me
Compatibility	—Trust based on background, values, approaches, interests and objectives held in common
Goodwill	—Trust based on the belief that other team members are concerned about my overall welfare
Predictability	—Trust based on the observation that the behavior of team members is consistent over time and in different contexts
Well-being	—Trust arising from the feeling that I have nothing to fear from other members of the team
Inclusion	—Trust based on the observation that other team members include me in their social and work activities
Accessibility	—Trust based on the observation that other team members share their true feelings and I can relate to them on a personal level

The Millennial generation have grown up in an era of freedom of choice. They can choose the time and place they receive their entertainment thanks to digital technology. They shop in supermarkets with thousands of products on the shelves and they shop online with an almost infinite choice. Amazon in the USA already has over 480 million products available through its website. So it's hardly surprising to find that they expect choice when they join an organization.

Digital technology has broken the ties between work and location. Employees now expect the freedom to choose when and where they get their work done. But to make this happen, leaders have to establish a truly trusting culture. They have to abandon the outdated concept that work is done during 'office hours' in their buildings and recognize that it is being done anywhere and anytime. And to make this happen effectively they have to trust employees to manage their own working patterns.

The traditional leadership culture lays down rules on how work is done. It runs on a 'management knows best' principle. It makes the decision on behalf of the workers, who are expected to comply. A well run organization has everyone doing their allotted tasks as part of the business process. Choice is limited and uniformity is good. 'Quality Management Systems' ensure that jobs are carried out in standard ways and are replicable. People are not trusted to make decisions outside of limited boundaries. Creativity is stifled and innovation is seen as damagingly disruptive.

The new culture for the Digital Age recognizes that individuals can be trusted to make decisions on how to do their jobs. Now it's 'Employee knows best' and control over when and where work is done can be delegated. People are given genuine autonomy, not just lip-service. Leaders are prepared to 'empower' their workforce by giving up power and moving away from exercising authority. People are trusted not to abuse the freedom. They are treated like adults, not like children.

It seems obvious that the way to motivate a modern workforce is to treat people with respect and assume they are responsible individuals. We have moved on from the nineteenth century society where people would know where they fitted into the 'class' system. Gender equality is now taken as the norm in most western societies. Equal opportunities are the basis of labor laws and increasingly organizations are championing diversity and inclusion. But many work cultures are still struggling to let go of the reins of the male dominated model of work.

One symptom of an outdated culture is digital overload. If people are not trusted to work their own way they are likely to fall victim to 'presenteeism'. The expectation from managers is that they can see their people and know that they are working. If they allow people to work remotely, perhaps from home, then how do they know that employees are actually working? So people are obliged to turn up to the office even when there is no compelling reason to be there. They may spend all the working day in a quiet office or tucked away at a desk, working on a computer or phone (which could be done anywhere with a good internet connection). Leaders who insist on their workers being physically present when the work could be done remotely show that they don't trust people to work on their own.

Furthermore, working in the office is open to interruptions. People drop by for a chat. Background noise is distracting. It's easy to get dragged into a meeting. And knowing that people are likely to be present, encourages ad hoc meetings. Not all of this is bad if it results in creative working and relationship-building. But often it means that time in the office is taken up with face-to-face interactions, leaving emails and other communications to be covered outside normal hours. And all that on top of the time taken to commute to and from the office. The overall result is to extend working hours into personal time.

One key to conquering Digital Overload must be to revisit our assumptions about work. Organizational cultures have been built up on the assumptions that work is divided into jobs and these are performed by people. So reward systems have been devised that are based on the time taken to do the job. Part-time workers are paid pro-rata. Someone seen to be working extended hours is described as 'dedicated' and 'loyal'. The 'hard-working' employee is praised. Consequently, we have cultures that subtly reward long hours. Replying to emails within a few hours, regardless of the time of day, is seen to be good behavior. Staying in touch over the weekend or on vacation is good for promotion.

To counter this, leaders have to recognize that work is performed for a purpose. They should agree on goals with their people and measure results against them. They need to reward output and outcomes, not input. This creates a high performance culture. It shows that people who meet their goals in the quickest time are the most productive, and as a result are rewarded for short hours not long ones. The best employees become the ones that leave early and have a balanced life. Ones that have to work long hours are considered to be failing.

This, however, is a challenge for many leaders. They have grown up in a macho environment, where managers brag about being busy and about the extra effort they have put in. They have sacrificed their personal lives on the altar of corporate success and are not about to admit that it was misguided. And they assume this is the inevitable way that organizations work. To be successful you have to dedicate your life to work. 'Work life balance' is something that applies to lower mortals, but they are above it. 'Wellbeing' is something that is good for more junior staff, but being a director is by definition a high pressured position.

Times have changed. Leaders need to earn the respect of their people. They also need to present an image to the outside world that shows they have a social conscience. Investors are looking for credentials such as caring for the environment as well as pure financial results. Corporate values now need to include the wellbeing of the workforce. Hollow statements about 'Our people are our most important asset' need to be backed up with real actions. Corporate values are not just convenient phrases that are put on a plaque on the wall. They are based on the behavior of leaders and the experiences of the staff working for them.

Organizations may say that they have a 'trusting' culture and then act in contradictory ways. A good example of this is the proliferation of email copies that clog up inboxes. It's very easy with digital technology to copy everyone you can possibly think of, just in case they need to know. As a result we have hundreds of unwanted emails, but we are obliged to sift through them in case some are of interest. Why is this happening?

To take a positive view, we might assume that the motivation in sending hundreds of copies is one of open communications and a willingness to share. However the opposite is also likely to be true. In a distrusting culture, people will send multiple copies to justify their existence. They can then refer back to the copies in the future and say 'I told you so' or 'You can't complain you didn't know what was going on'. In a trusting culture people are given freedom to get on with their work. In a distrusting one they are micromanaged. If your organization suffers from email overload it's worth asking why people are in the habit of copying everyone else. Is it a symptom of people justifying their existence, is it just laziness or is it caused by leadership behaviors that encourage misuse of digital technologies?

Leadership in the Digital Age

We are living in a world of rapidly changing markets, disrupted by digital technology. We no longer need to provide standard products from a mass-production process to provide affordable products and services. Traditional concepts of scale and efficiency no longer apply. Small companies can compete with the large ones and win, because they are more agile and can react to the market faster.

Organizations that were built for the age of standardization are out of date. We need smaller flatter units that can react faster. Functional stovepipes and layers of management get in the way of actions. Decision making cannot wait for bureaucratic procedures to take their time. Teams have to be empowered to take the initiative and achieve their goals without waiting for permission. The organization culture has to be actively managed by leaders who are visible throughout the business and not sitting behind a desk issuing orders.

We have ended up with outdated structures by building organizations out of jobs, laid out in an organization chart to show reporting lines and levels of hierarchy. But real organizations are based on work, not jobs; people, not positions; and collaboration, not reporting. Leaders must understand how cross-functional collaboration produces results, how informal teams develop and flourish, and how networks of people are forming and evolving all the time.

It's too easy for leaders to focus on the tangible factors and ignore the intangibles. Many have reached their senior positions by being good at understanding the finances, meeting the budget and issuing clear instructions. But the real world is run by people as well as systems. People who have opinions, feelings, emotions and their own individual needs. Too often individual needs are compromised by corporate needs. 'If my needs are ignored, then I will not feel valued and will be demotivated'. One successful approach to this is the work done by the psychologist, Shay McConnon and his 'An even better place to work'™ a self-managed culture-enhancing program designed to enable people to improve the quality of their work-lives. People will feel inspired and creative in the right atmosphere, or negative and troublesome in the wrong one. And how these people experience their working environment constitutes the 'culture'.

But just because culture is less tangible than the finances, that does not give leaders an excuse to ignore it. In fact, because it is less easy to define, it should be at the top of the list of priorities for leaders. Creating an environment where people are inspired to produce great results has to be the mark of a good leader. Running a business without caring about the culture is bound to lead to mediocre performance at best and failure at worst.

Reward Systems and Incentives

One key to managing culture is to examine the reward systems and incentives in the business. Some of this will be explicit, using conventional compensation systems, but much of it will be implicit. What behavior is incentivized, and which behaviors are rewarded in reality, regardless of the stated values and priorities? Managers may say they are concerned about the welfare of their people but many behave in ways that clearly contradict this.

Over the last 15 years, companies have moved from top-down, process-driven approaches to employee performance management (and annual appraisals) to a much more agile, continuous, feedback-based approach. Much of this is driven by the need to engage and empower young demanding employees, but it's also driven by a shift in management thinking. Employers are moving away from forced rankings and numeric ratings to regular check-ins, continuous coaching and agile goals. In the new world of management, employees want to be 'empowered' and 'inspired', not told what to do. They want to provide feedback to their managers, not wait for a year to receive feedback from their managers. They want to discuss their goals on a regular basis, share them with others, and track progress from peers.

Many organizations profess to have a 'performance' based culture, where they reward results, but reality is far from this. They may have annual bonus schemes but these are disconnected from the day-to-day output of the work. They may have abandoned the annual appraisal in favor of shorter term measures, but the financial reward schemes still tend to recognize effort more than results. So the 'hard working' employee gets recognized ahead of someone achieving the same results in a shorter time.

The result is a culture where long hours are accepted as the norm. Where it is a badge of honor to be working through the night to meet a deadline. Where being seen in the office late at night and sending emails whilst on vacation, brings thanks, not criticism, from managers. For a short term this might work, but soon employees recognize that they are living an unbalanced life and take action.

In many cases this means leaving the organization and then selling their skills back as an outside supplier. This gives the individual back control over their life and gives their ex-employer access to their knowledge and experience when needed. And the new contract will be based on supplying a service not just serving long hours. The result is an output based relationship that the employer found impossible to fit into their corporate culture.

Creating a Healthy Culture

Overall engagement levels are no higher than they were ten years ago. U.S. productivity since the launch of the iPhone has slowed, so the new tools and technologies we have at work are not making us more productive. Since 2000, American workers have lost an entire week of vacation, dropping average days from 20.3 to 16.2. A recent survey showed that 38% of Americans 'want to be seen as a work martyr'[60] yet 86% say it's bad for their family life. A Deloitte report[61] showed that 65% of executives rated the 'overwhelmed employee' an 'urgent' or 'important' trend, while 44% said that they are 'not ready' to deal with it. What on Earth is going on?

The problem is that many companies remain focused on 'point-in-time engagement' and have not yet pulled together the disciplines of performance management, goal setting, diversity, inclusion, wellness, workplace design, and leadership into an integrated framework. They have approached engagement as an HR program aimed at employees often in reaction to the annual employee survey. They have not looked at the total employee experience of work as part of their whole lives. In the same way that marketing and product teams have moved beyond customer satisfaction to look at the total customer experience, so HR needs to build strategies and programs to continuously improve the employee experience.

Key to maintaining an effective workforce is paying attention to to its health. This starts with the fundamentals of physical health. Employees need to work in safe environments where they are not likely to suffer injury or illness. They need work space that is appropriate for the tasks they are performing, so they can get on with the job without having undue physical hardship. Then they need to maintain physical fitness with work patterns that encourage exercise, healthy eating and adequate opportunity to relax.

We know that sitting at a desk for hours on end is not just bad for our bodies, but also our minds. Some research projects have shown that taking a break every 90 minutes improves productivity. Others have shown that a break every 50 minutes is beneficial. But many jobs do not allow this amount of freedom. How long can we continue to ignore the medical advice and continue with unhealthy working practices? Technology has a helpful role to play here though: an increasing number of people are being prompted by a buzz from their devices, whether Fit Bits or watches or phones, to stand up and take a walk after sitting for too long!

We need to rethink the design of work so it is not deliberately contributing to poor health. This is no longer an issue for the HR department, it is a matter of leadership strategy. If the culture of the organization is to value the wellbeing of workforce, it has to be backed up with policies and examples from the highest level. Just offering subsidized gym membership and healthy food options in the staff restaurant is not enough. Providing training on wellbeing is not very helpful if the leaders are clearly not following their own guidance. Offering employee counselling services for stressed staff is attempting to control the symptoms and avoiding the cause.

Stress has been described as the 'Health Epidemic of the twenty first Century' by the World Health Organization and its effect on our emotional and physical health can be devastating. In a recent USA study, over 50% of individuals felt that stress negatively impacted work productivity. According to a CIPD survey[62] in the UK, 38% of employees are under excessive pressure at least once a week and almost a third say they come home exhausted either often or always. Increased levels of job stress have been demonstrated to be associated with increased rates of heart attack, hypertension, obesity, addiction, anxiety, depression and other disorders.

Inevitably, some work is demanding and stretches the individual concerned. This in itself is not necessarily bad. Many people rise to a challenge and thrive with a target to reach. Where stress starts to appear is when the person feels they are out of control. If they feel under constant pressure and there is never any relief it is likely to become stressful. The UK Health and Safety Executive advises that 'A person can reduce the impact of high demands if they have high control over their work.' And 'The impact of high demands and low control can be reduced by having high levels of support, either from colleagues or from you as a manager.'

So leadership cultures that are seen to be supportive and give employees freedom are more likely to result in lower stress. Allowing people to control how they get their work done reduces the negative impact of stress. Smart working practices that empower employees will result in a healthier and more productive workforce.

Digital overload is a cause of stress because people feel out of control. The solution is to give them control over how they use the technology. They can choose when to use it and when to turn it off. They can see it as a tool to help them work more effectively. And they can use it to improve their work-life balance and not be an intrusion into their personal lives.

Key Learnings for Leaders

Leaders should develop cultural intelligence to able to navigate cultural complexity while maintaining digital fluency and relevance

A trusting culture gives employees freedom to control their lives and in return they give back improved loyalty and output.

Annual reviews are now evolving into continuous discussions to engage and empower young demanding employees

The disciplines of performance management, goal setting, diversity, inclusion, wellness, workplace design, and leadership should be pulled into an integrated framework.

Stress is a major problem and senior managers should be ensuring that the organization trains managers to recognize the signs and symptoms so that support can be provided and that there is a wellbeing program to counter it.

8

Creating an Engaging Environment

Matthias Mölleney and Sunnie Groeneveld

Engagement is at a low level across the world and the pressures from digital overload do not help. The Millennial generation has joined the workforce with different expectations about work-life balance and autonomy. Leaders must set the tone for the organization culture and design the employee experience for a positive work environment. New organizational models are emerging based on self-management and leaders need to keep up with the trends or risk losing key talent.

The world of work has fundamentally changed in the past decade. Among the most prominent drivers of change are the work habits and preferences of today's young professionals, now in their 20's and 30's, and the ever-pervasive digital economy. Both combine to present new challenges to managers and leaders across functions and industries.

M. Mölleney (✉) · S. Groeneveld
FutureWork Forum, Zurich, Switzerland
e-mail: matthias@moelleney.com

S. Groeneveld
e-mail: sunnie@inspire925.com

© The Author(s) 2018
P. Thomson et al. (eds.), *Conquering Digital Overload*,
https://doi.org/10.1007/978-3-319-63799-0_8

101

What remains to hold true, on the other hand, is that the world's leading organizations recognize as a strategic priority the need to bring in the most talented people, and make sure they remain engaged and grow with the organization. In this context, the concept of 'engagement' is more than job satisfaction. High levels of engagement mean employees are attentive and proactive, learn faster than others, regularly go the extra mile and stay loyal to the company. It is easier said than done, especially because the goalposts have moved in the past decade: the younger generation of professionals has different priorities and motivators than the previous ones, and many organizations are failing to recognize, let alone effectively respond, to their needs. What's more, if the Gallup league tables for employee engagement are any indication, leaders have some catch-up to do. The State of the Global Workplace[63] poll reveals that some 54% of workers in the United States are not engaged with their employers; Europe clocks in at 66%. This trend is echoed across most countries worldwide, where more than half of the employees consistently say they are not engaged. Overall survey results from Gallup show only 13% of employees worldwide are actively engaged and 24% are actively disengaged.

Add to this the impact of technology and we have a major challenge. Instead of the Digital Age making work more engaging, it is often doing the opposite. In theory the technology is freeing up workers to have a more balanced life and be more in control of how they work. In practice it is invading their personal lives and causing stress. The images of young vibrant start-ups populated with happy teams working in offices with sofas, dartboards and juice bars seem to be the exception. But many people hear of these examples and ask why their own company cannot be similar. They want to know why we are using technology to make our leisure life more enjoyable and not using it to make work more engaging.

Do these symptoms point to leaders' lack of recognition of the need to embrace new work practices? To the failure to accept that work habits need to change? Or that managers simply don't know how to lead the millennial generation of workers in an increasingly digitized world? These seem relevant questions to explore.

Millenials—What Do They Want?

Millennials, or 'Gen Y' are people born between 1980–1999. They make up 25% of today's total workforce and are set to take over the workforce by 2030, with a whopping 75%, according to the U.S. Bureau of Labor Statistics.[64] As they move into mid and senior-level positions across the global workplace, Millennials are having a (positive) disruptive influence on the world of work.

As every generation before them, Gen Y entered the working world with a fresh set of questions about why we work the way we do. More than any predecessors, Millennials want to be treated as equals in the workplace. They want to engage productively with others, make a positive impact and have careers of choice (not of desperation). Two-thirds of Millennials now state their organizations' 'purpose' is the reason they choose an employer.[65] In their quest for meaningful careers, they challenge the status quo, demanding answers from their employers on fundamental questions such as:

• Purpose: What is the purpose of my work? Is it making a difference in our world? Is my organization driving a positive impact for our planet?
• Hierarchy: Why do we need so many levels? Why can't we collaborate better across departments? Why can't everyone talk openly to everyone else, regardless of age and seniority?
• Flexibility: Why do we need an office? Why can't I work anywhere, anytime?
• Technology: Why can't we use state-of-the-art IT solutions at work? Why can't I bring my own mobile device and laptop to work? (What's a desktop computer?)

The next generation's senior workforce is entrepreneurial, cause-oriented, and more digitally connected than ever before. As the first generation to grow up with the Internet, they bring web thinking and habits to the office every day. And of course Millennials expect the technologies empowering their personal lives to drive communication and innovation in their workplace. Their paradigm is a workplace technology ecosystem that blends web, email, social networking, sharable Google documents, instant messaging, video-conferencing, blogs and wikis; to exchange openly and transparently with colleagues and customers, find instant answers to any question or solve problems collaboratively. Embedding these tools in the workplace more, enables this generation to instantly and naturally connect, engage, and work together with co-workers and managers. The end result? Higher productivity across the enterprise.

By now, many of the older Gen Y's will be in leadership positions as well as having young children. Hopefully they will be bringing new thinking into the leadership of their organizations. They represent change and of course some of today's best examples of innovative work environments come from companies started by Gen Y founders, or with a Gen Y majority in their leadership team, such as Jimdo. Others, however, come from forward-thinking companies, like Swissôtel which today is part of FRHI Group. Let's take a closer look at both of these examples.

Jimdo—Feeling Good at Work

Jimdo is a German software company with offices in Hamburg and Tokyo. It markets a 'build-your-own-website' toolkit that users click-and-drag to create your website with no technical expertise. To date, over 20 million Jimdo websites have been created. Founded in 2007 by Christian Springub (34), Fridtjof Detzner (34) and Matthias Henze (40) the company employs 200 employees from over 20 countries, most of them Gen Y. They have a good reputation in Germany, and have been recognized as the 'Best Startup Employer in Germany', according to the startup portal Deutsche Startups.[66] Jimdo can teach previous generation tech firms a thing or two about employee engagement.

There are two parts to how Jimdo creates an engaging work environment, a visible part and an invisible one. The visible part[67] is apparent the moment you step into their office in Hamburg: It boasts colourful design, an open work environment with kitchen and couch relaxation areas, and Chez Sam, an in-house restaurant run by a professional chef. Jimdo also offers childcare onsite and wellness opportunities, such as sports and running groups, or a washing machine to get laundry done during the workday.

The invisible part,[68] however, is what really sets Jimdo apart and explains why their employees are attentive and proactive, learn faster than others, regularly go the extra mile and stay loyal to the company. The founders put a strong accent on nurturing a 'we-feeling', that puts people first and hierarchy second. Having started as three friends in Fridtjof's parents' barn, the founders decided early on to create a position of 'Feel Good Manager' to ensure that even as the company grows, Jimdo would always offer an engaging work environment and feel like 'being part of a community, like you are going to work with friends every day.' The founders believe being a community of friends at work also translates into their products: 'We are certain that you can feel the excitement and passion that goes into creating our product. We know that behind every website there is a person with a story. Entrepreneurs, musicians, photographers, and people who are inspired to share their project online, thanks to us. Their success stories remind us, every day, of our journey. They also remind us of the simple truth that if you do what you enjoy, and share it with the world, you can achieve great things.'

Another important pillar of Jimdo's work environment is their adoption of the Kanban project management methodology, which helps to make collaboration better and protect everyone from juggling too many tasks at once. It is a very visual methodology and makes it easy to see what everyone is working on at any given time. This, in turn, helps ensure that people don't overload each other with tasks. In their job advertising Jimdo references Kanban and explicitly writes: 'We're not looking for worn-down workaholics. We want a team that is well-rested and excited to be here.'

The final 'invisible' pillar of Jimdo's engaging work environment is their commitment to being a flexible, constantly learning organization. They don't want their people to get stuck in boring routines, which is why they regularly make their teams change scenery to do project 'sprints.' These 'sprints' involve a small, interdisciplinary team working on a specific topic, usually off-site to break the daily routine. These periods can lead to new ideas, a stronger team spirit and even better collaborative efforts.

FRHI Hotels: Connecting Every Single Employee

FRHI Hotels & Resorts (FRHI) is a hotel management company that boasts more than 125 hotels and branded residential offerings in 35 countries with 45,000+ employees, many of them in the Gen Y age bracket. In 2014 top management decided to put a strategic focus on modernizing internal communications and improving employee engagement by creating a stronger sense of belonging across locations. This was particularly important because FRHI had recently rebranded and employees across the globe had little-to-no knowledge of their parent company. They often only felt a connection with their hotel site and to a lesser extent its brand (i.e. Fairmont, Raffles or Swissôtel). There was, however, no connection to FRHI as a whole. One chief cause was a lack of effective internal communication across hotels, time zones, cultures and languages. Further, although all employees were given an email account upon hire, many allowed it to expire because they didn't frequently work at a computer, for example, housekeeping teams or bellmen. This presented another challenge: approximately 15,000 of employees could be reached via email or the intranet while the remaining 30,000 could not be reached via digital channels.

Inspired by their vision to be the world's preferred hospitality company, the internal communications team launched FRHI Talk in 2014, a digital cross-devices communications platform that connected all 45,000 employees from around the world. The goal of the project was to establish an efficient, two-way digital communication channel that would help eliminate departmental silos and increase workplace collaboration. Today, most employees use FRHI Talk's mobile app, which has several news streams, instant messaging, document sharing, video training and more.

Andrada Paraschiv, Executive Director, Communication and Strategy says about FRHI Talk: 'Connecting 50,000 employees from 110 hotels globally and making them feel part of the FRHI family is not an easy task. Our 50,000 employees are separated by many miles, each working for one of the three brands, with little identification to the mother brand. It was important for us to find a way to connect the employees that was fun, surpassed the language barrier and was easy to use for employees in all positions.' Alexandra Zeifman, Project Manager at the internal communications team adds: 'Every day, our colleagues share celebrations, stories of excellence, every-day work experiences, and community involvement. We've noted that friendly competition between hotels takes place and employees now see what their sister hotels and regional offices are doing, something that they were not privy to before.'

Lessons Learned

What can other companies learn from these two examples when it comes to creating an engaging work environment?

Achieving high levels of engagement with the emerging generation of professionals relates to three issues: organizational culture (how leaders set the tone for a positive work experience; managerial style), managers' ability to accommodate the needs of talented young professionals (or their ability to acquire the skills to do it); and how to create a positive and productive physical workspace.

- Organizational Culture: Foster a sense of community. The borders between work and life are becoming more blurry and employees can increasingly work from anywhere in the world. Embrace this flexibility but make sure you focus on building a strong we-feeling so everyone still feels a strong connection to your company, no matter where they are physically.
- Leadership Style: Share openly and invest in digital collaboration. Manage your employees such that you encourage open information sharing and improve collaboration across hierarchies and departments. Work with the younger generation of employees to find the most suitable digital tools and then focus on rolling them out effectively. But keep in mind that it's not just about finding and buying a new tool. It's first and foremost about embracing a more collaborative leadership style.

- Positive Work Environment: Design the employee experience. Be just as meticulous about designing the employee experience as you are about designing the best customer experience. From the moment your prospective employees are interviewed to their tenth anniversary at the firm, ask yourself what are all the big and little things you can do to make the work environment a positive one?

As Gen Y professionals progress to more senior positions, smart organizations will adapt their company culture, technology ecosystem and work environment to the needs and expectations of this group, or risk losing them to more forward-thinking competitors. Consequently, the better employers become at creating an engaging environment around the aforementioned criteria, the more successful they will be in attracting and retaining Gen Y talent.

Rethinking Leadership

Building a modern, networked organization like Jimdo or FRHI Hotels requires a radical rethink for those involved. The idea that you can build a 21st Century knowledge organization with the tools and methods for designing hierarchical organizations, is as realistic as thinking that you could surf the internet with an electric typewriter, if you were persistent enough.

For those who think companies will always need to have traditional hierarchies, we found a very interesting project in Germany called «Augenhöhe» which means «on an equal footing». They produced a crowd-funded film featuring 6 companies which decided to be different. This includes creating workplaces where employees develop and unfold their full potential and use it for the good of the entire organization. The 6 companies are not crazy start-ups, they are well established SMEs like allsafe Jungfalk in Southern Germany and Premium Cola, a beverage company in the North of Germany, but also big brands like Unilever Germany and Adidas AG. They have explained the project in a video on the internet at http://augenhoehe-film.de/en/film-2/augenhoehe-film/.

Are you feeling inspired and wonder how to get started in shaping the architecture for a 21st Century organization? Observing businesses made by Millennials is a start. Looking at how people working from home organize their work and lives also offers inspiration.

A focus on collaboration over hierarchy is a common feature of the networked organization. Where the corporate dinosaurs of the past (and many still roam the landscape) spent tons of energy on internal politics, or building and protecting their silos, networked organizations excel at collaboration, consultation and thrive with flat management structures. They place the highest value on team performance, quick and agile feedback cycles, such as 'learning before, during and after' practices, over celebrating individual success.

Have you heard about Freitag[69] the company which gives old truck tarps a second life as trendy messenger bags and sells them all over the world? The Freitag brothers decided that being CEO or other C-level executives and working in traditional power patterns is not what their company needs to develop further. Reaching a next level of economic performance is not enough, what they want is a company which integrates and involves everybody across the entire company in creative and decision making processes. They looked for a suitable concept and found Holacracy, a new peer-to-peer 'operating system' that increases transparency, accountability, and organizational agility.

But there is a danger in trying to adopt a self-organizing system without having the right culture to support it. Adding a system like Holacracy to an existing organization can be seen as constraining individual freedom and forcing people to work in ways they do not find natural and adds to the existing workload. One company that has been heralded as an example of Holacracy is Zappos. Tony Hsieh, their CEO has said 'So we're trying to figure out how to structure Zappos more like a city, and less like a bureaucratic corporation. In a city, people and businesses are self-organizing. We're trying to do the same thing by switching from a normal hierarchical structure to a system which enables employees to act more like entrepreneurs and self-direct their work instead of reporting to a manager who tells them what to do.'

Zappos have struggled to implement the scheme, despite having a very supportive CEO and a culture that already was anti-status.

If they are finding it difficult then its unlikely to be a magic solution that can be bolted on to conventional leadership practices. Most of the companies are still far away from flat hierarchies and agile ways of collaboration. Here's a comment from a veteran sales manager at a traditional German company: 'I spend 40% of my time on the defensive against torpedoes fired by my enemies in-house. Another 40% firing my own torpedoes back. With the remaining 20% for further development of my weapons systems.' A bit exaggerated, perhaps, but the silo mentality still reigns supreme in many organizations.

The old thinking is dying a slow death. As the Millennials occupy more senior positions in the professional workforce in most countries, the last century's corporate thinking will start to fade more quickly. But how soon before 2030 can we expect to see the last twitch of the dinosaur's tail?

Networked companies work in the way they do, not because they subscribe to a different management model, but for a far more practical consideration: survival. Or to take a positive view: the continuous search for innovative ways to improve the business, delight the customer, and have a happy and productive team. Leaders of networked companies see hierarchy as useful for defining clear and transparent structures, but also as a severe constraint on reacting quickly to evolving markets and customer needs.

What do tomorrow's leaders want? How do they see the world of traditional corporate thinking? In a series of interviews with European young professionals by the FutureWork Forum a young university graduate from Estonia said: 'Why should I ask somebody with a job title if I can also ask someone who knows the answer?'

So, the managers in the new, light, structures need to be network leaders. Networks are dynamic and flexible; they don't respect hierarchies and departmental boundaries. For the workforce's new talent, the norm is cooperation, self-motivation and problem solving. A network staffed with the right people needs effective network leaders, and this kind of management requires a light touch.

Millennials say that they perform best in their ideal conditions. Among these are: flexible working patterns; work from home, and outside 9–5; clear targets to deliver on; a fun and flexible workplace and opportunities for professional development and advancement.

To be sure, staff need to embrace the company culture. But they also contribute to it. So just as a young professional will be asked to adhere to the organization's processes and core principles, managers will need to adapt to this new normal.

Some get it. Others will need re-skilling to move away from command and control to facilitation and motivation. Presentism still prevails in many organizations. Why? Partly because there are many old-style managers who are not comfortable, or effective, managing people who aren't physically present in the office.

A Millennial professional will say that she is always there, on-line, delivering and interacting on assigned tasks. A good network leader will recognize this and motivate teams by managing by results. Face-to-face is vital, the young generation may say, but not really needed or productive for every minute of every day.

Of course, there is no obligation to embrace the super-modern work style. Organizations don't have to do adapt radical decentralization; they can require staff to be on-site every day. It will be interesting to observe how more traditional thinking organizations fare a decade from now, as the networked groups continue to evolve and respond to professional needs and market changes. Most interestingly, perhaps, what kind of talent will the traditional and the networkers be able to attract?

How, then, to adapt traditional management systems to perform well as network organizations? If modern companies still need a management structure, its legitimacy will need re-establishing. In the era of post-shareholder-value approaches, the sole decision of the owners about the use of executive board members is inadequate. It needs augmenting with a sharp focus on influencing and engaging other stakeholders, especially employees. Extreme forms such as democratic election of CEOs by the workforce are known, but these practices will remain marginal. Social media are emerging as useful business communication, learning and knowledge sharing tools. Corporate intranets use community spaces à la Facebook, or micro-blogging platforms such as Yammer as meeting places for thematic groups and technical teams to capture and share project work and learning. Wikis and blogs have been part of the knowledge sharing landscape for years. Top management needs to upgrade its thinking in this area and confirm that social media platforms are a part of normal business practice, replacing e-mail for more efficient forms of online collaboration. Why? Well, because that's the way our world, and the generation of soon-to-be-40-year-olds, works.

Performance management can also be adjusted to meet networked cultures and practices. One possibility would be the StaRHs concept proposed by Heiko Fischer,[70] where employees can award stars (StaRHs) as individual recognition for special support or other performance to those colleagues with whom they work within the network. The StaRH is continuously updated so that everyone can track who is earning how many StaRHs for what. This helps to demonstrate the value of the network. If customer, business partner, and supplier reviews could then be integrated in a further phase, this would come quite close to a stakeholder-driven selection of management teams.

This evolving landscape calls for middle managers to become network leaders. But embedding new skills in these professionals will require some retooling. Created to ensure communication between top management and employees, this middle layer in the corporate structure has largely disappeared in most organizations, replaced by faster communication using digital communication processes and tools, and encouraged by lighter performance management structures.

The technical expertise required of today's managers has risen so sharply that in many cases it receives more emphasis than their leadership skills. This can be the impetus to turn managers into network leaders. And this is exactly where the future of middle management lies.

How do network leaders lead their employees? In these self-organizing structures, there is rarely a fixed leadership relationship between employee and supervisor. Rather, leadership is assigned by project, task force, or even network. In this fluid and distributed world, the top-down methods of the past are less effective. In demand today are methods for building and stabilizing networks.

Beyond Leadership

'Beyond Leadership', an instrument proposed by Patrick Cowden, helps transform management methods for network organizations. Cowden, former CEO of Dell Germany and former European Head for Hitachi, left the rat race of the CEO's career, realizing that the management of large companies could not continue as it was.[71] He saw first-hand how many corporate leaders were at their wit's end after decades of budget cuts, restructuring, job cuts and motivation campaigns, and were no longer able to mobilize employee enthusiasm, better planning and deliver long-term goals. Instead, they saw more time and energy invested in managing more stringent budget details, process optimization, and delineating departmental boundaries: all these rationalizations seem to achieve the exact opposite effect.

Cowden personally experienced what happens if you focus more on tools and processes than on people. In his book 'Neustart'[72] he argues that people achieve more together if they are not working next to each other or with each other, but instead FOR one another, if they feel connected to each other, and if they are committed to jointly agreed goals. The infighting and selfishness described above have no chance if the employees have such ties. Cowden calls this 'the power of connect'.

These methods work well, but in most cases, are not sustainable as they are not sufficiently integrated into the day-to-day working life. Beyond Leadership combines the lessons learned from good team-building approaches, trust-based management and positive leadership. The Beyond Leadership Model is designed to help groups work together to design and implement strategies, manage change, or solve a difficult task.

The first and most important step of the Beyond Leadership Model is called Connect. It is designed to build a solid bridge of trust between individuals, because they learn much more about each other than in any other classical team building exercises. While this step focuses on the individual, the participants discover in the second step the common values and beliefs of their organization. Phase 3 defines the goals of the organization and phase 4 the individual contribution of the participants. All steps are being held in the same groups of three and the with the same process of four minute inputs and two times one minute positive feedback. One of the factors which differentiate this model from other approaches is the consequent focus on positive feedback and on equal contribution from all participants.

In this context, Beyond Leadership is makes new connections between employees, cutting through hierarchy and departmental affiliation. For networked and self-managed companies it is a practical method for creating new management structures, and an innovative tool for network leaders. Deutsche Bahn, the German railway company is currently evaluating how Beyond Leadership could help them to overcome traditional barriers against effective collaboration. Companies like Swisscom, the leading Swiss telecommunication company, are using this approach to support the implementation of new and fluid organizational structures.

A true pioneer of new ways to lead a company is Ricardo Semler. As CEO of the famous Brazilian company Semco, he explains his radical ideas in his TED talk 'How to run a company with almost no rules'[73] and in two best-selling books. His ideas might be too radical for many traditional companies, but the stunning success of Semco is a good reason to listen carefully to what he is saying about democratic leadership, i.e. leaders are being evaluated and elected every six months by their subordinates, about his salary model which entitles every employee to define his own salary and many other ideas which make Semco an employee and customer centric company.

Other examples of self-organization are quoted by Frederic Laloux in his book, 'Reinventing Organizations.'[74] He points out that we need more enlightened leaders, but we need something more: enlightened organizational structures and practices. The pioneering organizations researched for his book have fundamentally questioned every aspect of management and have come up with entirely new organizational methods. Even though they operate in very different industries and geographies, the structures and practices they have developed are remarkably similar. It's hard not to get excited about this finding: a new organizational model seems to be emerging, and it promises a soulful revolution in the workplace.

Of course, there are various other concepts, but they all have the same goal: developing and strengthening the collaboration between employees in agile organizations. Functional groups need to be broken up into real teams, which means they are smaller and work more empowered. Leaders leave their desks and learn to perform hands-on leadership. This change also calls for new forms of reward, the change from individual bonus systems to team rewards and profit sharing. We must say good-bye to the annual employee performance appraisal and replace it with continuous feedback and quarterly updated goals which are transparent and shared publicly. We will see a radical reduction of the number of classical job levels to motivate people to strive for results and learning rather than just promotions. Our companies will become development areas, not only for customer focused solutions, but also for the employees themselves. That requires a new approach of leadership which tries to connect people rather than make them rivals.

Asking what makes an employer truly attractive, a recent study from Universum[75] shows that graduates' highest listed value has not changed over the past number of years; it is work-life-balance. Working in an atmosphere of trust-based collaboration is one of the two most important factors of work-life-balance. The second is the grade of autonomy over personal working time. A bus driver who works eight hours is double as productive as a fellow colleague who drives a bus for four hours, but the essay of a journalist who spend eight hours writing it is not double as good as the essay of another author who invested only four hours. There are many jobs where working time is relevant to measure the performance, but the number of jobs where this does not make sense, e.g. the knowledge workers, is increasing. In these cases, it is sufficient to define quantitative and qualitative goals and not the length of the working time to be spent.

This is the reason why the Belgian Ministry (FPS) for Social Security has implemented an innovative new working model: Each employee has the full autonomy when, how and where he works. He has a work package assigned with a clear number of cases to be solved, a quality target (maximum number of mistakes) and a customer satisfaction target. The organization does not care about the working time which means the employees decide how fast or slow they would prefer to work. The results after three years of experience show an incredible number of 95% among the employees who like this new freedom better than the old system with fixed working times.[76] On top of that, customer satisfaction went up 60% and the output by 30%. Since then, the Ministry is also one of the most attractive employers in Belgium in its area. A striking argument for this kind of increased flexibility.

As a summary, we can notice that engagement in a new world of working requires a mind-set change in various dimensions. We need to redefine leadership as a service to employees, enabling and encouraging them to work in flexible network-like structures, to build trust-based connections and to take responsibility over their work-life-balance. This will lead to a reduction of stress and overload, a better use of technology and most important a gain in happiness. Only very few organizations are as radical as the Belgian Ministry for Social Security which changed the title of the Director of Human Resources to Chief Happiness Officer. Leadership needs to take responsibility for the welfare of the workforce, and Human Resources Management needs to support this by leaving the ivory tower of administration, introducing new ways of collaboration and a new flexibility for employees.

Key Learnings for Leaders

Millennials are questioning traditional work practices and leaders need to respond to them or risk missing out on young talent.

Organizations need to develop positive work environments or face an inability to recruit and retain the talent needed to succeed.

Employers of all sizes are now paying attention to employee engagement and designing a positive work environment.

An open culture where a sense of community prevails, knowledge is shared and employees are empowered will deliver the best results.

People working for each other in a fluid organization structure will collaborate effectively.

Working in an atmosphere of trust-based collaboration and autonomy over personal working time will reduce digital overload.

9

Wellbeing and the Workplace

Peter Thomson, Andrew Chadwick and Larissa Hämisegger

The workplace has evolved with technology to reflect the needs of the users. It has now extended out of the building to many other places. Office design has changed to allow for flexible use and there is now a focus on making the space support healthy work patterns. Wellbeing has now become a strategic issue for leaders, contributing to business success. Digital technologies are becoming addictive and employers have to have programs in place to counter this.

P. Thomson (✉)
FutureWork Forum, Henley-on-Thames, UK
e-mail: peter.thomson@me.com

A. Chadwick
FutureWork Forum, London, UK
e-mail: ac@chadwick-international.com

L. Hämisegger
FutureWork Forum, Zurich, Switzerland
e-mail: larissa@unumondo.io

© The Author(s) 2018
P. Thomson et al. (eds.), *Conquering Digital Overload*,
https://doi.org/10.1007/978-3-319-63799-0_9

The Evolving Workplace

Historically, office work has been associated with a fixed location. By definition it had to be performed in an 'office'. From the Uffizi building in Florence in the 1500s to the open plan office of the twentieth Century there have been evolutions in design. But the principle of workers sitting at fixed positions remained firm.

Now in the twenty first Century this is no longer the case. 'Office work' has evolved into 'knowledge work' which can be performed in a variety of settings. Digital technology has freed people up from being attached to a desk but instead tied them to a laptop, tablet or smartphone. However, the overwhelming majority of people still have a place they can identify as their workplace. When we leave home in the morning, 'I'm going to work' still means 'I'm about to travel to my workplace', so work and place are synonymous.

There have obviously been developments in office space throughout history. Introduction of the elevator created skyscrapers. Introduction of better lighting and air conditioning allowed people to work in different settings. Since the 1950s the office has been evolving with the introduction of open space, open plan, cubicles, and co-working spaces replacing the classic 'walls and door' office. Although individual closed offices still exist in many organizations, recent surveys show that the vast majority of the professional and administrative workforces in developed economies work in some form of shared space: the figure is some 70% in the US, according to one survey[77].

The term 'modern office' conjures up images of large, colourful spaces (preferably with an atrium) buzzing with activity, collaboration, group problem-solving and constant innovation. The visionary managers who put these spaces in place trumpeted their benefits for profitability and efficiency through better use of infrastructure costs; and for the quality of professional interaction through increased collaboration between teams, leading to increased innovation, and value for the organization. But are they suitable for today's working patterns?

Open Spaces

Recent business media reports predict the beginning of the death of open spaces, and provide anecdotal and qualitative evidence of to show why open space is not the best approach to increased worker wellbeing and productivity that many have suggested. One Danish study concluded that people working in the open spaces were more frequently ill and absent from work on sick leave. It was not foreseen that collaboration extends to the sharing of germs in an open space[78]. A sneeze, it seems, goes a long way to affecting corporate performance in some open settings.

Likewise, other studies highlight employees feeling that noise and continual distractions in open workspaces are a drain on productivity, and a negative impact on staff motivation.[79] Another survey found that collaboration does not happen spontaneously, nor is it needed every minute of every day. This report found that open space workers polled were exchanging on many things, and not a lot of work collaboration.

Yet open space is still the predominant model for the office. There are obvious financial drivers behind this but a balance has to be made between cost, productivity and optimal employee engagement. If people are stressed because their work environment is not suitable, the lost productivity will cost the business much more than the savings in real estate expense. So what is best?

Flexible Space

As flexible working started to take off in the 1970's, the approach to the workplace became more fluid. Technology was evolving that allowed people to keep in touch when they were not in the office. The introduction of the mobile phone in the 80's and smartphones in the 90's freed up office workers from the fixed phone line. But the major change has emerged in the twenty first Century with the availability of broadband, wifi, social media and apps for everything imaginable. It's not surprising that the workplace has struggled to keep up with the options now available to the knowledge worker.

Flexibility in space and time for work has resulted in a more flexible approach to office design. This started in the 90's with the growth of 'hot-desking'. Organizations realized that their desk occupancy was not much more than 50% and they were paying expensive city rents for empty space. So for people who were not in the building every day, it was obvious that they should share their desks. This worked well for groups such as sales reps who were out meeting customers, but was not popular with people who were in the office more often. The loss of an identifiable base can be unsettling and be a cause of stress.

Researchers at the Centre for Research on Children and Families in the UK[80] found the lack of a desk for social workers to return to after often difficult home visits added to their sense of 'emotional disorientation', left them without a physical 'secure base' to work from, and could reduce chances to interact with colleagues. The report said: 'Increasing uncertainty into a role, which is already dealing with high levels of uncertainty with their cases, will increase levels of stress. Reducing opportunities for working and meeting with colleagues takes away an important buffer of stress in this profession.'

Imposing desk-sharing on unwilling employees is a likely cause of unrest. People may feel less of a sense of belonging and welcome in the office. In many cases they end up occupying the same space on a daily basis anyway and come up with plans to keep hold of 'their' desk. In contrast, designing flexible space in consultation with the users can be an engaging experience and employees feel ownership of the result. How the allocation of space is managed can also affect employee attitudes.

SpaceTime (the Space you need for the Time you need it), another name for Hot Desking, has been with us since its inception at Chiat Day in California and Andersen Consulting in London both in 1991.

Take up was slow and confined largely to the consultancies, but now it is widespread and even Government departments are allocating space in decimals of desks at 0.7, 0.8 or 0.9 of a desk per person.

There are fundamentally two ways to manage SpaceTime: Reservation and Free Address. Free Address is 'first come first served' and as the name implies is like booking an aircraft seat. Interestingly the airline industry started with Free Address, which resulted in crowds of anxious people at the gate. Now almost universally they have a Reservation process to allow for orderly boarding. Working space is moving this way with the growth of booking systems in flexible offices.

Activity Based Working

But we are now moving beyond the simple SpaceTime model to a much more flexible approach to the workplace. This is known as Activity Based Working (ABW). In this system employees choose to work in the space that best supports their activity at the time. So, someone wanting an informal meeting with one other person may choose a coffee lounge environment. Or if the meeting is more formal they may want to sit at a table. If they want to work quietly on their own they can find a secluded corner, or if they want to experience the buzz of a busy team they can sit alongside a colleague.

The important factor here is that the employee decides. They are not told where to work, they find something that suits the task and also suits their mood. They feel in control and that reduces stress. And the logical extension to ABW in the office building is to include other work locations as well.

So a full ABW scheme will include the home, the coffee shop, the train to work, shared hub space and any other place that work can be done. It is now common to see cafés with customers on laptops and phones, and many people are working whilst travelling. So the workplace can be almost anywhere if employers allow it. But many employers do not trust their staff to choose their place of work. They insist that they come to the office regularly whether that's the best place for the task or not. And by doing this they are contributing to the Digital Overload problem.

Leaders need to set the right example and pass on the right messages. If they make it clear that work can be done anywhere and they trust people to manage their own work patterns, then people will feel empowered. If they insist that people have to come into the office to do their jobs, then they will not be getting the best return from their people or their real estate. Of course there are times when people have to be in the building to meet others face-to-face, and some tasks may only be performed in the office, but sitting at a desk sending emails to the person at the next desk makes no sense at all.

This might sound like a recipe for chaos but in practice it works well. People do not just disappear off, never to be seen again. They choose times and places for their work that fit in with the rest of their lives. But they respect the need to get the work done in collaboration with others. They come to the office for meetings and team events, and they catch up on emails from home if that works for them. The result is a lowering of the stress associated with digital overload. Smart leaders measure the output of their staff, not the hours they spend in the office.

Wellbeing in the Office

For many people there is no choice of workplace. They have to be facing customers in a shop, serving drinks in a bar or treating patients in a hospital. There may be some choice on when they get to do their work but it cannot be done remotely. And even those who do 'desk work' will have to spend some of their time in an office. So it is important that the hours we spend in the workplace are as productive as possible.

Sitting at the same desk for hours on end is not good for physical or mental health. Yet that is what we still expect employees to do. Slowly, however, this is changing. Office design is now encouraging people to move about, in conjunction with Activity Based Working. Sit/stand desks allow people to stand up and not sit all day. Stairs are strategically placed to encourage their use instead of elevators. Conference rooms with no seats get people standing for meetings and reduce meeting times as well.

Modern buildings provide an environment with temperature, light and noise levels carefully planned. They use the atrium to bring in as much natural light as possible and use windows to provide views outside. Workplace designers consider color and the use of plants to produce a more relaxing environment. All this helps to reduce the stress of working in an office but it will only be effective if it is accompanied by leadership behaviors that encourage a healthy lifestyle. It's no use providing a gym if it's never used by busy executives. It's pointless providing bicycle racks and showers if nobody cycles to work. It's a waste of effort designing healthy menus for the staff restaurant if the Directors don't have time to eat there and get sandwiches in meetings.

In an attempt at introducing a 'Wellbeing' program, employers may provide employee counselling services, advice on drug and alcohol abuse, health checks and subsidized gym membership. They may provide free fruit and massages, but this doesn't make them a healthy workplace. At best these are dealing with the symptoms and not addressing the causes of stress. At worst they are used as an excuse for increasing workloads and putting more pressure on work-life balance.

Wellbeing as a Leadership Strategy

Digital overload can be minimized if leaders implement a Wellbeing strategy. This is more than just a set of HR policies, it is an approach that shows how an employee is valued more than just as an asset to be used, but that they are valued as a person, an individual. To truly achieve a healthy workplace, employers need to ensure that their culture, leadership and people management are the foundation on which to build a fully integrated well-being approach.

According to the CIPD 'An employer's approach to employee wellbeing needs to be sustainable and linked to both the organization's corporate strategy and workforce needs, and integrated within every aspect of its people management activities.'[81] They point out that there is often a gap between rhetoric and reality. Leaders say they value their people and then ignore the high pressure, stressful working environment they have created. But they are also missing the benefits of a healthy workforce.

Research commissioned by the Health Work Wellbeing Executive[82] in the UK, found 'a wealth of evidence' in the academic and non-academic literature suggesting a positive link between the introduction of wellness programs in the workplace and improved business key performance indicators. The available literature suggests that program costs can quickly be translated into financial benefits, says the report, either through cost savings or additional revenue generation.

It also points to Corporate Social Responsibility as a key measure on company leadership. Many multinational companies include wellness in their annual reports on social responsibility. Of the 20 largest multinational companies, 75% publish corporate responsibility reports online, of which 93% emphasize their commitment to improving the health of employees. This reflects the view of the World Business Council for Sustainable Development, which states that corporate social responsibility is about 'improving the quality of life of the workforce and their families as well as of the local community and society at large.'

It is well known that work related stress is a major issue at national and international levels. The ILO describes it as occurring when 'the demands of the job do not match or exceed the capabilities, resources, or needs of the worker, or when the knowledge or abilities of an individual worker or group to cope are not matched with the expectations of the organizational culture of an enterprise.'[83] They also point out that technological advancement and the emergence of the internet have led to many changes and innovations in work processes, making the boundaries between work and personal life more and more difficult to identify. The same report sates 'Workers might feel that staying connected longer and responding quickly is a sign of good performance, continuing in practice to do their job at home and outside working hours.'

So, against this background of increasing public concern about mental health at work, what can leaders do about it? Firstly they need to raise visibility of the issue by discussing it openly as a business problem. Instead of ignoring the facts, employers need to take responsibility for their human resource and maintain it in top condition to perform the work expected. Investing in the wellbeing of this resource will bring returns that flow through to the bottom line. Conversely, pushing the resource beyond it's capacity to cope is irresponsible leadership, and makes no business sense.

The Investors In People (IIP) standard in the UK has a Health and Wellbeing Award[84] for employers. This addresses three areas; Physical Wellbeing, Social Wellbeing and Psychological Wellbeing. To achieve the advanced level in the standard, leaders need to show they 'take ownership of health and wellbeing in their organization, actively driving and contributing towards positive outcomes.' And to achieve the top level they have to show that 'Health and wellbeing is fully embedded within the culture of the organization.'

If a responsible leader found that their organization culture was driving people to drugs or alcohol, they would want to take decisive action to sort out the problem. Yet that's what is happening with technology. Internet Addiction Disorder is now a recognized psychological condition and technostress is now a subject of serious research. And even if the use of technology at work stops short of being an addiction it is still demanding a disproportional amount of attention. Having to cope with the 'firehose' of information, described in the technology sections of this book, crowds out any time for creative thinking and reflective decision-making.

One solution that is now being tried by organizations is mindfulness. It is too easily dismissed as some strange Buddhist meditation practice that has no place in the serious company. But companies such as Google point out that in the last century nobody paid much attention to physical fitness as being a concern for employers. Now they are using mindfulness as 'fitness for the mind'. It makes business sense for employers to invest in improving the quality of brainpower in the workforce. This also aligns with the wishes of the next generation of workers who are looking for quality of life, with work integrating into a meaningful and satisfying existence.

The point is that wellbeing is not a separate policy or program. It has to be built into the leadership culture. It's not just running a few stress awareness courses, it's looking more closely at the way people are managed to see where the problem starts. So leaders need to ask questions about how pressurized their employees are on a day-to-day basis. Do they encourage unhealthy working patterns through poor job design and task allocation? Do they give freedom to employees to work in their own way, or are staff forced to work long hours at times that cause family pressures? Do they allow technology to take over people's lives and cause digital overload?

Key Learnings for Leaders

A well designed workspace is critical for healthy and productive staff.

Activity based working gives employees choice over where they work and supports flexible working programs.

Wellbeing is a strategic issue and should be visibly supported by top leaders.

Stress is a serious problem and investment in mental health is as important as investment in physical health.

Wellness is a matter for Corporate Social Responsibility.

10

Actions to Mitigate Digital Overload

Michael Staunton and Michael Devlin

Given the current challenges that 'digital' brings to the workplace, it is likely that we will see more interventions from governments, organizations, and from people acting to taking control of their situation to navigate the digital world. How to avoid being caught unprepared for the digital deluge, and keep pace with this fast-changing world? For leaders navigating the ever-changing digital society, the question is how to achieve the parallel goals of high productivity and staff motivation. Leaders need to review their talent strategies to get the most out of the millennial workforce.

M. Staunton (✉)
FutureWork Forum, Winchester, UK
e-mail: michaelstaunton@mac.com

M. Devlin
FutureWork Forum, Brussels, Belgium
e-mail: devlinmichael1@gmail.com

© The Author(s) 2018
P. Thomson et al. (eds.), *Conquering Digital Overload*,
https://doi.org/10.1007/978-3-319-63799-0_10

Introduction

This chapter reflects on the 'always on' syndrome that digital overload creates for some organizations and their professional staff. All organizations face the same overload issues, but some are less affected by it. Is the difference due to policies and guidelines, management edicts to switch off email on weekends and go home on time, and discouraging staff to checking constantly on nights and weekends? The reviews, interviews and desk research done in compiling this chapter point to one core factor that sets more serene company styles apart from the chaotic and burnout-prone workplace; and a rather old-school one at that.

At the organization level It seems that leadership style goes a long way to reducing the risk of overload and burnout. This is not new management theory. It's simply that effective leaders need to 'walk the talk' and lead by example. This will show that overload is not a requirement and that there are practical approaches to navigate the digital tsunami we all face, to maintain higher productivity and motivation and avert the risk of burnout. We also see that governments are preparing and, in some cases have already intervened, to address email use in the workplace and at home. Finally, we look at what practical actions each person can take to improve their situation, and what are the key issues that need to be considered to address staff motivation and performance in today's digital world.

While governments and individuals can (and certainly need to) respond to the digital challenge, we argue that leadership style is more effective than solid policies and company rules. In the end, leadership style affects management style, affects staff behavior, affects customer service levels, affects brand image, affects quality of work, and ultimately shareholder value. This issue is much bigger than 'email overload'. And it is the leader that is directly responsible for affecting this situation, or not.

The Radicati Group[85] estimates that the number of email users worldwide will grow to 2.9 billion by 2019. In 2015, the number of emails sent out per day was 205 billion they estimate that by 2019, that will have grown to 246 billion.

This means that professional staff could easily spend every minute of every day 'doing email'. Faced with these facts, senior managers, responsible for boosting productivity and profitability will do well to better understand what is behind this stream of information, and what email communication is optimal for, and where it is a break on organizational effectiveness.

In the past decade, there has been a lot of debate on the optimal use of email, with some research, and a number of opposing views. The trend for modern organizational development thinkers is that the world is moving toward knowledge and learning communities that interact in bespoke digital spaces. This has the merit of getting away from chit-chat and constant distraction of mails continually pinging into the inbox. A number of examples illustrate companies where this is working well, and also show some spectacular failures of new digital community platforms.

Of course, there is no silver bullet. Generally speaking, the companies that have switched on the new million-dollar platform with the directive that 'this is how we are working now', beat a hasty retreat to good old email months later, as staff did not warm to the technology (more likely, to the directive). Companies that walked the talk seem to have had a considerably better experience. These leaders recognize the benefit of new platforms, and that it is a change management exercise not a technology solution. So it is personal engagement by them in promoting and using the new technologies that will drive a successful shift in new digital thinking, and ultimately a better workplace.

Having said this, it is not at all clear that email is the root of all evil and that every company should transition out of this medium to new platforms. A recent study by a well-know global health care company looking to improve the effectiveness of its digital marketing channels, found that most potential customers remain interested in receiving information by email.

So the jury is still out. It's horses for courses. And leaders need to understand what is on offer and craft a digital engagement strategy that is best for their information ecosystem, internally and externally.

Hard Policies and Legislation

This section examines legislation and policies in organizations, which are emerging as important factors in the debate on digital overload. Some of the pressure to focus on this issue comes from trade unions and employee groups concerned that working hours will increase, as people do more of their work outside of the office, often in their own time, through email. Another area of the increasing importance is the move toward wellness polices in many workplaces aimed at improving employees' physical and mental health. A recent study (2015)[86] found that checking emails outside of work time increases stress levels and reduces wellbeing.

So how have governments responded? In January 2017 a new French law came into force that requires companies with 50 or more employees to establish hours when staff should not send or answer emails. The goals of the law are include making sure employees are fairly paid for work, preventing burnout by protecting private time. In this case private time is seen as holidays, weekends, and after working hours.[87]

David Morris writing in Fortune suggested that in recognition of this several European corporations have made attempts on their own to reduce the risks of burnout and overwork for employees by restricting email usage. In 2012, Volkswagen blocked all emails to employees' Blackberries after-hours. Daimler took the step of deleting all emails received by employees while on vacation. Again from a government perspective the German labor ministry enacted a limited ban as far back as 2014, by prohibiting managers from calling or emailing staff after work hours, except in an emergency.

Ursula von der Leyen the Labour minister set out rules over the use of work-related mobile phones by her own department's staff as a way of encouraging similar behaviors in German organizations.[88] Her view was that technology should not control people's lives and that there should be rules for accessibility outside of work time. The principle being that people shouldn't be accessible out of work time except in particular agreed circumstances. Part of the justification was to avoid burn out in the long term.

The principles of von der Leyen's 'rules for exceptional accessibility outside of individual working times' state that 'No one who is reachable through mobile access and a mobile phone is obliged to use these outside of individual working hours.' Other commentators also shared this view; that managers shouldn't call or email staff outside of work except in emergencies to save from the stress of being constantly on call. Nick Bacon Professor of HR management at Cass Business School saw the intervention in Germany as leading the way on progressive modern work practice. His view was that there is a need to adopt clear policies to ensure work-life balance and for organizations to achieve wellbeing and productivity aspirations. Ann Francke, chief executive of the Chartered Management Institute and author of 'The FT Guide to Management', echoed the view that managers need to be able to build relations in their families and be able to switch off. In her view being always on is a form of 'presenteeism' and managers need to work out what is reasonable and avoid the need to constantly check for and send messages.

Yet at the same time the rise of the digital world of work seems inexorable. Pierre Nanterme, Chairman and CEO of Accenture gives an example of how companies in the future may well focus more on building internal social media and collaborative technology tools.[89] Accenture employs 300,000 people in over 100 countries around the world and adopted a radical solution by not building a physical HQ and achieving savings as a result. In fact the leaders of the company physically meet only once every quarter and as a consequence the leadership of the company is closer to clients and employees around the globe. Instead of an HQ, Accenture invested in internal social media and collaborative technology. The organization as a result is totally 'digital' and all governance and meetings are 'virtual'. Nanterme argues that there is positive response from Accenture employees as they are 'digital natives'

In this scenario described at Accenture there are potential benefits for the individual in companies that adopt a digital approach. The question appears to be; 'can digital natives and the rest of us cope with Digital Overload?'. Alexandra Samuel argues that the fears of digital overload may be overplayed and that individuals might miss the opportunities in accessing the breadth of the digital world available to them through LinkedIn, Twitter, Facebook etc. She recognizes that through social media individuals are surpassing the Dunbar constant. Dunbar argues that cognitive limit to the number of people with whom one can maintain stable social relationships, in which an individual knows who each person is and how each person relates to every other person, is 150 stable relationships.

Samuel argues that people can effectively manage digital overload by changing their approach. By learning to focus; using guidelines; applying different work practices: and the use of digital tools. Samuels's belief is that digital overload can be redefined as an abundance of opportunities rather than as a problem. In fact digital overload can be converted into a professional asset.

Throughout this book, you will read that the nature of work is changing due in a large part to changes in technology and that there needs to be response to those changes. One issue that will need to be explored is what motivates people, especially in the digital age. Dan Pink, an expert on motivation, highlights an important perspective when we look at what motivates us all, especially when we are looking at high-level work. He shows how the assumption that financial incentives can motivate people to higher performance is flawed.[90]

In fact Pink argues that financial incentives can actually become a 'disincentive' for higher-level work and that this case has been proved by research based analysis. Generally, work is becoming more high level and as work gets increasingly automated through the application of new technology the likelihood is that this will only increase. We are now seeing impressive applications of Artificial Intelligence. One example is the potential growth in driverless technology that is forecast for the near future.

Pink identifies that there are three core motivators. Firstly, he describes Autonomy, which is the desire to be self-directed. This means people need a high degree of freedom to set their own work direction and also the methods and circumstances of their work. Pink talks about Apache, Wikipedia, and Linux as examples of companies where people who were often already in paid jobs gave up their discretionary time **for free** to help develop solutions which are now used by many organizations.

The second motivator is Mastery, which in simple terms is the desire to get better at stuff. For this element of motivation, the argument is that people generally like to do things well and the get better at things they value, so opportunities to grow and to develop and excel at their work are intrinsically motivating. Finally, he refers to Transcendent Purpose. This is the notion that people need to feel that their work has meaning and value and they will choose to invest themselves in activities that they consider to be worthwhile. He also quotes the vision of Skype, which aims to be disruptive in the cause of making the world a better place.

Pink also uses the example of the Australian software company Atlassian to illustrate the type of intervention that organizations may use to motivate their people. Once a quarter on a Thursday afternoon the company says to its developers that for the next 24 hours you can work on whatever you want. All that is asked in return is that whatever the developers come up with is shown to the company at the end of that 24 our period. It is a fun meeting and it turns out that the one of the outputs of this approach has been a whole array of fixes for existing software and many new ideas for new products, which would never have emerged if this initiative had not been undertaken. As Pink says, the idea is that Atlassian 'get out of the way of their staff' in order to tap into their discretionary effort and creativity. Cleary new approaches to motivation will be required and there will similarly be a shift towards approaches like coaching rather than 'command and control'.

As work changes increase, how we deal with staff and assess them also needs to change. Lucy Kellaway in a recent article talks about how Accenture and Deloitte are making substantial changes to the annual performance appraisal process.[91] Kellaway comments that Deloitte has come up with four things, which its own managers are asked every quarter about each member of their teams. Kellaway paraphrases these questions as:

> Does this person deserve lots more money?
> Do I like having them on my team?
> Do I think they are likely to screw up big time?
> Would I promote them today?

She also comments that Deloitte will insist that all its managers check in with the people they manage once a week. She comes up with a simpler suggestion; that organizations only hire managers who can manage and are good at telling people how they are doing, not once a week but all the time. For her, the appraisal system is a crutch for poor managers.

In a recent TED talk *'Don't fear intelligent machines. Work with them.'* chess grand master Garry Kasparov, who was beaten by IBM supercomputer Deep Blue in1997, makes his case.[92] He concludes that, historically, humans have competed with machines, while today humans need to work with machines.

He says that the triumph and success of machines is underpinned by human success in creating the machines. Soon machines will be taxi drivers, doctors, and professors as the Artificial Intelligence of machines continues to progress. Rather than compete with machines Kasparov believes that what is needed is a better man-machine interface to support a more useful intelligence.

Coaching for the Digital Age

Digital age technology is impacting the way people develop current and future leaders. The application of digital platforms is likely to revolutionize the way organizations view and purchase development in traditional sectors such as Executive Coaching. Coach Connector is an interesting new initiative creating a global online executive coaching platform that allows organizations to assess and measure coaching contribution to the organization, the manager, and the coachee.

The technology behind Coach Connector aims is on-line and 100% trackable and measurable, with a unique ROI tool for executive coaching. Using a live dashboard the aim of the platform is to streamline the coaching process by:-

1. Measuring Return on Investment, the effectiveness and the value of the coaching investment.
2. Saving huge amounts of organizational time through online tracking of past, current and future coaching programs.
3. Speeding up the matching process and get senior managers to engage more.

Coach Connector members can now measure any executive coaching programme, using an ROI tool—The CoCo Index™. This is a proprietary on-line calculator designed to enable HR Managers to calculate the

<u>perceived value</u> (using numerical metrics) of their investment in executive coaching for high achieving talent. The aim is to use the on-line tool to be used by both coaches and organizations worldwide to measure the effectiveness and demonstrate the value of coaching. The ultimate aim is to develop trust between organizations, purchasers and providers of coaching.

The platform has video profiles to make it quicker and easier for the coachee to decide who they might want to select for an initial chemistry meeting; logs dates of the meetings and coaching sessions; and automatically triggers reminders for participants, to log mid-point reviews, and feedback updates at the end of a coaching program.

Founder of Coach Connector Fraser Murray says 'Our singular goal is to create a better paradigm than that which currently exists in the still conservative off-line world of executive coaching and streamline the job of corporate HR professionals tasked with running executive coaching programs. Like Airbnb, we want our business brand 'The CoCo Index' to become the industry standard, a verb in the lexicon of executive coaching, synonymous with 'making good leaders even better'.

Practices and Leadership Style

Now let's hear from the practitioners. The best performing companies are guided by policies and standard operating procedure. But many seem to not have policies that address email and digital overload.

Too much email and the 'always on' culture that lead to burnout are symptoms. The root causes of anxiety and stress linked to digital overload are indecisive leadership, and managers who fail to embrace the new world of digital work and transmit a clear expectations and practices to their teams.

The investigations done in compiling this chapter show that leadership style is a key determining factor in improving workplace conditions related to digital overload. This includes staff motivation, productivity and peace-of-mind for staff. And it is senior management's responsibility to clearly articulate 'how we work'.

Leadership styles that improve productivity and reduce burnout:

- Improve work quality and work-life balance
- Address issues caused by increased stress
- Make organizations as competitive and high-performance as possible

To be sure, every HR manual presents guidance on the importance of taking time off, using all your holidays in the calendar year (that's what it is for); policies for medical or maternity/paternity leave; and statements about wellness and work-life balance. But explicit statements and rules on dealing with the digital deluge faced by every professional today, are not elaborated in detail. Perhaps this is because leaders don't know what to do. Or that there is no real solution and this is something we need to live with.

The examples cited here show how forward-thinking leaders in two intergovernmental organizations set the tone for a balanced digital work-life relationship for their teams. But this also shows how employees have the luck of the draw. They may end up with a manager who does not value downtime, or who feels that 'always-on' is a fact of life and can't be managed. This could be because the manager faces the same requirements from their superior. Or maybe they have no solution and are loathe to ask for help and advice.

Clear policies without leaders walking the talk, don't solve overload. But neither do good practices by some and not by others in a policy-weak environment. It cuts both ways.

Email is the Symptom, not the Problem

Email is certainly a threat to efficiency, says David Allen, a consultant and the author of 'Getting Things Done' and 'Making It All Work'. According to Allen,[93] email overload is a symptom of a larger issue: a lack of clear and effective guidelines for professional practices.

If an organization has ambiguous decision-making processes and people don't get what they need from their colleagues, they are more likely to flood the system with email and meeting requests. People then get mired down in their backlogs, leading to even more email traffic from frustrated co-workers trying to follow up.

Allen cites one of his clients with an average backlog of 3000–4000 emails. When he finally cleared the backlog and stayed on top of his inbox, both his email traffic and meeting load decreased.

His colleagues got the direction and input they needed so they didn't need to hound him for follow-up on pending work issues. 'Email, handled well, reduces meetings; and meetings handled well reduce emails,' Allen says. Taking the time to reply now to an email query will save twice the time in the future. Writing in the Harvard Business Review,[94] Amy Gallo echoes the message that the email issue is a symptom of deeper organizational dysfunction.

Take a Break

As email is such a constant presence in our lives, it can be refreshing to periodically disconnect from all things digital. Some do this on annual leave. Others take a deliberate 'email sabbatical'. One academic had an auto reply saying: 'Due to the need to focus on my work over the next six months and the increasing amount of emails I receive, I will not be answering any mails over the following six months…' Faced with the imperative to deliver quality work, professionals develop their own coping strategies. But clearly, this university researcher has a specific work situation. What manager or project coordinator could take six months off email to 'get organized'?

Allen advises that it's a good idea to untangle yourself from the world of intense digital engagements, just to prove you're not hopelessly addicted and get some fresh air. But this strategy isn't for everyone. If you're constantly preoccupied by what you're missing, on-line, you may be better off spending time manage your digital affairs, he counsels.

The UN's World Food Program: Ensuring Work-Life Balance in an 'Always On' Sector

By definition, the UN's World Food Program's (WFP) work is 'always on'. This agency is on the front line, delivering food to populations in the world's worst conflict and crisis situations. The WFP teams' work is driven by urgency and rapid response to crises where millions of lives are in danger: from Afghanistan to South Sudan, Yemen or Central African Republic.

While this is may not seem a relevant case for solutions to digital overload, the WFP emergency response culture offers a clear view of how complex information and logistics environments can be effectively managed, while ensuring wellness in the workplace.

Enrica Porcari is Chief Information Officer and Director of Information Technology, overseeing the work of some 1000 staff at WFP. She sees a distinct difference between 'always-on' and the urgency that many teams experience that is fueled by chaos and poor planning.

WFP does not have explicit policies for weekend emails and related issues. She sets the tone with a work style for a motivated team that responds effectively to global humanitarian crises, and avoids burnout. 'Emergency response is part of our DNA. It's in our employment contracts. And the leadership has to demonstrate what is expected. If it's urgent I say it. But everything is not urgent. And it is not acceptable that something becomes urgent for many, due to poor planning by a team member; especially as a recurring issue.'

Porcari is very sensitive to this. So policies are useful, but leadership style is what sets the tone.

Here's how it plays out for her team at WFP: 'I don't expect colleagues to work on Saturday or Sunday, so I don't send email on the weekend. Emails sent late and on the weekend sends wrong signals and people will feel obliged to react.' Like all senior managers, she confesses to keep abreast of issues on email over the weekend: it's the nature of the business. But she is mindful of the effect that a mail from the director has on employees when sent after hours. So she typically sends mails in a batch on Sunday evening.

In this case, a leadership style seems to be a stronger motivator than digital engagement policies. And digital overload is probably the area where we can try to legislate, but in the end the managers who can best motivate teams and navigate the ever-encroaching digital invasion from work into our private lives, will be able to attract and keep the best.

The week-end email syndrome fuels the 'I'm here!' syndrome, where some staff members pop up reacting to emails with a comment or acknowledgement. But where is the substance in these exchanges? It's the same as staying in the office late to make an impression.

Porcari comments: 'We have an agreement to respect people's personal time. I don't abuse it because I'm the boss, this is counter-productive. All this behavior counts in having a well managed and motivated team. If the boss is on email constantly and staying in the office late, this sends stress signals to staff, even if they tell the team not to engage after hours.

So in the WFP, the culture can best be described as 'well-managed always on'. While there is no explicit digital overload engagement policy, the solutions are a mix of leaders 'walking the talk', of good sense approaches to dealing with digital deluge and very clear rules for wellness and R&R for field staff. They are explicitly expected *not* to be available after weeks of intense activity in crisis situations.

She summarizes this organization's best practices: 'Staff is king; wellness of staff is king; and the leader's style sets the tone for staff wellness and productivity.'

Sharat Kumar is Director of Corporate Services for the International Center for Agricultural Research in the Semi-arid Tropics (ICRISAT), a global research center with some 1100 professional and scientific staff working across 10 time zones of Asia and Africa. One of his leadership roles is for global HR. He offers his perspective on strategies for coping with digital overload and how management can set the tone for a more productive workplace.

As a leader in your organization, how are you managing the issue of 24-hour availability?

I'm not available 24-hours and I don't expect my staff to be available 24-hours. In emergency cases my staff and I are available to handle the crisis. In my view, it is not correct to be available for 24-hours nor to expect staff to be available. If your organization expects you to be constantly available, I would rethink if this is the right place to work. Email and other modern ways of electronic communication systems came into being about two decades' ago. These were considered business enablers, designed to make our lives easy. But very quickly these tools have taken over our lives, without our realizing their impact. I wonder if a professional can be effective at work if they are continually overstretched.

Do you have policies or guidelines for being on-line and off-line. If not, should you?

We don't have a written policy or guidelines. But, as a senior leader I am expected to be available 24/7 for all important issues that cannot wait. As a leader, I need to prioritize and determine the importance of issues and act accordingly. As a rule of thumb, I don't respond to emails (1) where I'm copied (2) with more than one person listed in 'To' and (3) Reply All. This criterion does not apply to emails received from my manager.

Unless it is urgent and requires immediate attention, I don't expect my staff to respond immediately or on holidays. In the case of exceptions, I request for a response but with an apology.

Do you see the expectation of continual availability as an issue for your organization, that needs to be managed? Should leadership set the tone, or is this an issue that each employee should figure out and manage themselves?

Yes, this is an issue and senior leadership must set the tone and clearly communicate expectations, do's and don'ts and email behavior. Change in culture is needed and must be modeled from the top. Organizations cannot let staff figure out how to address these issues and manage themselves regarding digital overload issues.

Does 'email' etiquette work: for example, guidelines for expected response times, CCing people, etc.?

Any number of guidelines will not work unless the desired culture is modeled from the top. Very quickly people in organizations realize what is expected from them when the style is clearly set my leadership. I certainly do not expect my staff to access or respond to emails all the time.

What is your advice to CEOs on this issue, especially in the light of organizational efficiency and how to be an attractive employer that needs to catch and keep the best talent in a competitive job market?

Model the behavior and set an example. Encourage staff across the organization to follow good email practice. If not, this will impact on the productivity and morale of the organization.

Anything else you would like to add?

Digital addiction is a new and rampant disease that will increase if we are not aware of its impact on our lives. It leads to severe withdrawal symptoms for some people when they are deprived of data/Wi-Fi access. A number of leading hospitals have started outpatient and therapy centers to address digital addiction. Unfortunately, tech screens have the same effects as Class A drugs. It is high time that organizations realize this and address this as a serious matter, before an increasing number of people face burnout or end up in therapy.

Harnessing Experience and Knowledge

We've said that there is no silver bullet to solving digital overload. So rather than search for solutions, let's focus on best-fit technologies and approaches that improve productivity. Email won't go away. It has its place in a productive work environment. But this resolutely 90's technology is being used for a host of business tasks for which it is quite ill-suited. Take the scenario of a group of engineers exchanging emails for group problem solving. As the email string gets increasingly involved and information-rich, participants may compile this into a report or summary, or individual members may file the results in their own folder structures, or shared folders, as the discussion continues.

Management efficiency gurus might smile at this example, saying this is the way we worked in the past, and things have moved on. For many innovative teams, things have moved on. But in the majority of organizations, this kind of information chaos remains the rule.

Is it really so important *how* we work, so long as we reach a good result? Well, yes. Smarter ways of organizing and exchanging information waste less time and effort. They help teams get more quickly to the point of making sense of rich information exchanges to learn and innovate together; to make a better process or product; to beat the competition. So groups that are good at this spend less time wading through masses of information and mail exchanges, and more time meeting their business goals and producing innovative solutions for their customers.

French tech giant, Atos is one company that has come up with a unique solution for knowledge sharing and organizational learning. Looking at what he saw was a massive waste of productivity caused by internal emails, CEO, Thierry Breton, launched a program to phase out this medium for internal communication. Replacing it by thematic information groups where learning and experiences on the company's core business themes is exchanged and stored.

Interestingly, this lucid view of how productivity can be improved, by focusing on the right digital technologies for the right tasks, is not the brainwave of a Silicon Valley whiz kid. Breton comes from classic business structures: former chief executive and chairman of France Telecom, served as France's minister of economy, finance and industry for two years and lectured at Harvard Business School. At Atos, his data on staff behavior revealed that most of the young people hired were using Outlook and email for the first time when joining Atos Today's generation lives on social media and mobile Apps. He commissioned a study to see how many internal emails the company's 80,000 employees receive. The average was over 100 emails per person per day. Further analysis showed that the staff found 15% of the messages useful, and the rest a waste of time, spending 15 to 20 hour a week checking and answering internal emails.

The solution was to reduce internal email over four-years, moving toward a complete ban. As Breton explained in 2012: 'When we no longer have internal email we will have fantastic new tools; a cloud computing environment, social networks, instant messaging, micro blogging, document sharing and knowledge community platforms. These offer a much better knowledge exchange for an information technology company.'[95] By 2014 Atos had reduced internal email by 60% and created training programs for over 5000 managers to teach them how to lead their departments and projects in a zero-email environment.[96]

It's not that communications have reduced across Atos. Employees post in the company's internal thematic communities 300,000 times a month, and those messages are viewed nearly two million times monthly. Most importantly, all of those views are by choice. People are using instant messaging and social media tools as part of the Atos global initiative, 'Wellbeing at Work'.

Atos is not alone. Many global companies are moving to micro blogging or thematic discussion groups to focus their information exchanges and learning. The hope is that with more structure and focus, digital overload will reduce and interactions be better managed.

So, in addition to leading by example on how and when to interact digitally, leaders also hold a critical responsibility to emulate good practices of embracing new information platforms and the communication styles that are needed to capitalize on them. 'Walking the talk' means leading the team into future ways of working. And to do this, they will have to modify their habits; getting to blogging, posting in discussion forums, tweeting or chatting, commenting on others' posts, making podcasts or short video comments. This is the way the professional world consumes information today.

The shift to new learning platforms and ways of exchanging is inevitable, especially as this is how millennials prefer to interact. Keeping abreast of digital economy developments is becoming a continual change management effort for today's leaders. Some may be concerned that we are simply creating digital overload 3.0. But this is unlikely to happen if we understand the landscape and what tools and practices can help to navigate it.

Key Learning Points for Leaders

Governments are likely to take decisions to intervene, as in France and Germany, and organizations need to look critically at their work context and culture, to decide what action they need to take.

Organizations need to adopt new digital approaches in order to keep up with the changing competitive landscape.

You will need to decide what your digital strategy is, as it will certainly lead to you revise or change your talent strategy.

We will all need to equip ourselves for today's digital reality. This means understanding the power of social media and learning platforms, and being able to focus better; to cut through the surging waves of information and develop our own digital techniques and tool kits.

Leaders must change too. As Tolstoy wrote, 'Everyone thinks of changing the world, but no one thinks of changing himself'

11

Technology-Based Solutions

Cliff Dennett and Mike Johnson

In this part of the book, the idea is to offer some practical ideas on how to address the impacts of technology on your workforce, find some respite from that ever present 'firehose' of information we looked at in Chap. 5 *and begin to get a meaningful grip on the realities of trying to deliver business success in an always-on world. In looking for solutions, we need to look at the technology itself but perhaps more usefully; our attitudes towards technology and how we use it.*

For much of our working requirements, the technologists have brought us all the information we want, largely when we want it. Most of the time we can get what we want, right away. As explored elsewhere in this book, this often leads to the destructive notion that just because

C. Dennett (✉)
FutureWork Forum, Birmingham, UK
e-mail: cdennett@mac.com

M. Johnson
FutureWork Forum, Lymington, UK
e-mail: mike.ajohnson@michaeljohnsonassociates.co.uk

© The Author(s) 2018
P. Thomson et al. (eds.), *Conquering Digital Overload*,
https://doi.org/10.1007/978-3-319-63799-0_11

we can get what we want in real time, we need to respond also in real time.

However, not everything has to be done right now and very quickly. Human beings benefit from time to reflect. Books aren't written in a single stream of consciousness, overnight, in a single session. They take months of exploration and reflection. All things have their own pace and their own level of urgency. All people have their own thinking and working speeds and their own sense of what is urgent.

Here are two broad approaches to the leadership challenge:

1. replace the existing IT systems causing the stress with alternatives, or
2. use these existing IT systems in better ways.

Whichever approach we take, digital leadership requires recognition and focus. I am going to examine ways to look at both possibilities, hopefully giving you the opportunity to not only revisit the issues you face in dealing with the tidal wave of digital overload but to create some options that you and your co-workers can adopt and embrace.

Replace the Existing IT Systems Causing the Stress with Alternative IT Systems

This is a short section because I believe we are in a bit of a no-man's land currently. It's difficult to determine whether we are wrestling with the inadequacies of the current crop of communications technologies while waiting for something better, or our approach to leadership hasn't caught up with the technological advances described elsewhere in this book.

If we look at the kinds of technology managers use in the workplace and consider the very real motivational needs of a workforce, current communication systems do feel lacking and even the near future doesn't look that bright. The promises of virtual reality (VR: where you don a headset and dive into non-existent, but highly real-feeling virtual worlds), augmented reality (AR: where a device such as a smartphone or smart glasses overlays additional information onto the real world, a little like a head-up display) and other deeper biological technologies haven't really created value to date for the average organisation struggling to fight the information fire-hose.

Even the latest messaging platforms such as Slack, still basically blast the user with a constant stream of information, information that is still delivered in arguably tired ways (mainly text and imagery).

Significantly different ways to process information are on the horizon. Immersive data rooms are coming, resembling Star-Trek-like 'holodecks' that allow users to immerse themselves in a virtual room of data. New visualization techniques will provide easier ways to interpret complex data sets and help leaders make better decisions. Deeper biological connections will speed up our interfaces with technology, directly connecting mind and machine. All of these are certainly revolutionary, but none of these are likely to help you over your next 1–3 year delivery period! You need answers to digital overload now and VR won't be helping you any time soon.

Closer to home, modifications to today's applications are appearing that do seek to minimise the interruptive nature of 'epoch 4 technologies'. I recently came across a change to Apple's ubiquitous mobile operating system, 'iOS' that removed the little red 'notification count' from the icons of apps on your home screens. You know the ones; they constantly remind you that you have 300 unread email messages or 20 social media notifications. Instead, the typeface of the app name becomes gradually more heavy/emboldened, the more the notifications are stacking up, offering a slightly more subtle way to remind you to check your messages.

In another experiment, a company implemented email credits which meant employees could only send a certain number of them per day. The sender could attach a number of credits to each sent email, indicating the importance to the reader attached by the sender. In essence, this provided a quick sanity-check, or second thought to be given to the distribution and importance of messages, before sending.

These are all well and good, but while the technologists are trying to make IT less interruptive, for me, the answer is not a technological one, but a cultural one. To improve the way we use technology, we must first change the way we perceive it. Frankly, we all need to grow up a bit!

Using Existing Systems in Better Ways

There's an *emotionally intelligent* approach to using IT, that is applicable whether you work in an organizational environment or at home. Drawing from the world of executive coaching and loosely based on CBT (cognitive behavioral therapy). This has at least two levels; an individual one and a cultural one.

From an individual's perspective, the first thing to do is to recognize that your relationship with the systems you are using is not inherently healthy. Many people find themselves, through no fault of their own, in a conflict-driven adult/child relationship with technology, where the technology feels like the adult and the user like the child. Many people 'have to respond' to 'so many emails' every day that they 'can't keep up' with 'the day job'. Others have trouble responding to emails because of the 'demands to maintain an active social media presence'. Digital presenteeism has become a bane rather than a boon.

As when dealing with any negative relationship, the first stage for getting any kind of relief (or respite), is for any victim to admit to themselves that they are suffering. This needs to be followed by a further recognition that they can actually do something about how they feel and actually do something positive to negate these effects.

We tend to divide our activities between our digital lives and our real-world selves in the language we use. We talk about being on-line and off-line or on and off the grid as though technology has somehow created different versions of us. There is certainly a very real difference between the bits (or bots?) of us that exist offline and online. The main difference is that whatever you write or post online is frozen in time, distributed without further control by you and re-recorded over and over again. In real life of course, you can change, adapt or revise your opinions.

Has this really changed who we are as human beings? Has technology changed us, or simply amplified some basic human needs that leadership theory and practice have been trying to address for decades? Are there new problems at work to be solved as a result of technology, or have the same problems always been there but now have a global magnification that is impossible to ignore?

In an example known as Kant's Tiger, the German philosopher, Immanuel Kant traces human behaviour back to how we perceive things rather than the things themselves. He illustrates this by imagining a meeting with a seemingly dangerous animal:

1. I see a tiger
2. I think I'm in danger
3. I feel afraid
4. I run

Kant's proposition was that (3) and (4) are a result of (2) not (1): i.e. that you can change your emotional response and subsequent actions by revisiting how you are perceiving the world. Suggestions why 4 could be the wrong response, range from: The tiger may be caged; you might be an experienced tracker or tamer; the tiger may just have fed or be on its way to look after cubs or it may be tracking a larger prey and not interested in you. In any case, running is probably the least best survival technique!

Taking the analogy a stage further, you or one of your co-workers can choose to view electronic communications in a similar way: (many have admitted to us in interviews around this subject, when it comes to email and keeping up with technology, they do have a tiger by the tail!)

1. I receive an email
2. I'm in danger of being seen as a slacker
3. I feel anxious to respond as quickly as I can
4. I cc or bcc ten other people, just to make sure

Actions (3) and (4) are driven by (2), not by (1).

In a way, technology and in particular email, amplifies the often irrational feelings of self-doubt and under-confidence. This is of course very much job-dependent. Your internal systems may be actively set up such that email is a very important process tool. For instance if you are in a sales role and the primary method for receiving leads is through email, then of course it is important to respond in a timely manner. This however is very different say from a departmental manager or more senior leader whose job it is to get things done.

The key point here is to recognize when you have become a slave to the machine (rather than the inverse), because it's most likely that the machine has happened accidentally and is certainly not the best thing to be a slave to, for you, or the organization. Bosses don't really want people to respond to email, they want the job done, whether that's through email, Snapchat, Facebook, letter or stagecoach.

Once you recognize this (and there is of course a cultural aspect to this that is bigger than the individual, and we'll come back to this), then coping strategies start to clarify. Once you realize you need more of an adult-adult relationship with technology then you can start to implement some really simple but highly effective tactics, putting you back in the driving seat. Here are some very simple examples:

1. Turn off all notifications. Most mobile apps and many online web services try to turn on notifications by default. This means that every time a new email, Whatsapp message, LinkedIn or Facebook post arrives, your phone pings and 'echoes' around in your pocket. Turn them OFF. If people really need you, they'll call or knock on your door. Most updates you get are general information about things you have expressed an interest in and are not time-dependent. As part of the curing, getting to grips strategy, they should in no way distract you and can wait!

2. Don't charge you phone by the side of your bed. This seems very obvious, but how many times have you either (1) been distracted by flashing lights, buzzing and pinging during the night and (2) woken up for some other reason and immediately reached for your phone to check the time, only to notice a list of new notifications on a nice bright screen that wakes you up and sucks you into two hours of mindless social media activity? Leave your phone downstairs to charge, making sure you have switched it into do not disturb mode (those pings and vibrations really shout at you from other rooms in

the dead of night) and buy yourself one of those cheap old-fashioned (and on-trend) alarm clocks to keep by your bed.

3. When at work; if you're using Word, shut everything else (especially email and social media) down. If you're using email, shut everything else down. Just because apps can run in the background, it doesn't mean that they should do. Every ping, every pop-up, every vibration is a trigger that switches your mind from the task in hand and it may not get back on task for another 20 minutes. Accept that multitasking may not be the best way to get the most things done and instead become more sequential with your work. Get as far as you can with one task, before switching to another.

4. Unless you are extremely, incredibly, amazingly well-organized and disciplined then don't use email as your to do list and don't use email as the way you keep track of what you have asked other people to do. I have met a few people with highly structured email file structures for archiving emails (you can create folders that exist beyond your inbox you know) but I can count them on one hand (at last I would if I had time to allocate a hand away from answering emails!). Email was never designed as a task management tool or to-do list and deferring emails to be answered later rarely gets the job done. The greater volume of emails you receive, the least effective it is likely to be as a way to organize your life.

5. Taking a digital break once per week, or per month and certainly when you go away really works for enhancing your well-being. The hardest thing is shutting those notifications down, closing that email app or shutting off the work inbox. Once you've done that and picked up a book, gone to the pub, had a waterski lesson or hiked that mountain, you very quickly forget and start living in the moment. No need to go completely off grid, but taking some structured off-grid time is the electronic equivalent of taking a break to walk over lunch or timeout in the garden.

We're not talking about *disconnectionism* here. This isn't a reversion to the 70's Californian call to 'tune in and drop out'. The goal is not to demonize technology but to recognize when the adult-child dynamic is taking over from a more healthy adult-adult one.

No serious colleague should ever be sending mission-critical or life-threatening information via any kind of messaging service. Of course, customers need responding to, reports need compiling, everyone has deadlines. Proactively manage these and turn the distractions off. You probably wouldn't have the TV running when you were trying to concentrate on reading or writing a report or analyzing some finances, so why have more intrusive services running?

There may be some organizations that have directives around minimum email response times, or amount of social media activity an employee should engage in for the good of the company but I doubt there are many! However, one of the biggest reasons for the feelings of digital overload through work is a perceived culture of immediate response; that somehow everything that comes into an email inbox simply must be responded to and that response should come as fast as possible. Culturally, this needs fighting against.

Any attempts at de-digitizing you and your organization will only probably work if there is an impetus or incentive to do it as a group (one-on-one cutting off your digital umbilical cord is unlikely to succeed). But what you do need to succeed as a group or even organization-wide is to adopt coping strategies that will allow the best to be harvested and the wasteful to be discarded.

As a leader, you are key to defining and reinforcing the culture of your organization. Those brand or employee values that your marketing and human resource departments spend so much time reinforcing, need to be applied to your employees' digital lives as well.

Let's say your organizational values are; trust, integrity, respect and ownership (most organizational value systems are like these; yours probably aren't far off) then these need to be applied to how your company perceives and operates its digital life. Your company needs a digital policy in the same way it needs any other one. Here's a made up example of how these values could be applied to digital:

TRUST:
—Because I trust my colleagues, I don't need to record everything down and capture it in an email audit trail.

INTEGRITY:

—I uphold both the spirit of our processes and culture and will not use email to 'cover my backside' or to 'gang up' on colleagues.

—I will spot instances where others are using email in an ineffective manner and respectfully help them to see a better way (I will NOT do this using email!)

RESPECT:

—I respect my colleagues and their ability to do the right thing. I will not copy in people who do not need to know and will take particular care about recording things electronically that may be sensitive to individuals.

—I will avoid sending emails out of work hours as this can create additional stress for colleagues.

—I respect that my colleagues' time is equally valuable and will consider what messages I need to send to whom so as not to abuse that time.

OWNERSHIP:

—Before I send an email or post a status update, I will think about why I am doing this and whether I am owning the issue and will avoid diluting my ownership through copying in people who don't need to know.

—I will consider whether I need to pull together a group of people to discuss something openly, before automatically turning to email.

OK, so these are a made up list and I'm sure you can put better words down against your own core values but the point is that no one has probably considered doing so in your organization. Even attempting to do this with your HR or Brand departments will start sending a clear signal across your organization that your company takes very seriously any technology that hinders, rather than helps, the personal development and wellbeing of its employees.

Too often, if a company has a digital strategy, they are almost always market-focused, answering questions such as: 'How can we reach out to a wider audience' or 'How can we use digital to cut costs'. In the same way that you have both marketing and HR strategies, you need a flipside to a digital marketing strategy, i.e. a digital employee strategy.

Following the mantra that if you look after your employees, then they'll look after your customers, that's real digital leadership. So what does an employee-focused digital strategy look like? As with any strategy, it should be specific to your organization so it's hard to generalize but here are a few principles you might want to start with (and of course tailor to your own needs). Some are more tactical, some more big picture:

1. When specifying new IT systems, ask the vendors how the systems help combat digital overload. This is likely to be met with a fairly blank response, but if everyone starts asking the question as part of the buying decisions, software developers will start building these considerations into the core design of their systems.
2. When you implement new systems, consider principles for how they should be set up to minimize digital overload. These could include adding filters or channels to split information up, principles on their general use and guiding principles about what kinds of response times are expected.
3. Make sure these questions are discussed at senior management level, perhaps even at the board. Digital culture forms part of communications culture and should therefore be a significant strategic consideration for any company.
4. As part of setting culture, for instance during inductions, ask all employees to ask themselves the following questions before sending anything electronically to anyone:
   IF we didn't have email, instant messaging, social networking etc ...

   a. ... would I still send this message and how differently would I create it?
   b. ... would I copy this message to those I am putting on 'cc' or 'bcc'?
   c. ... how else would I communicate this message to make it more effective and welcome?

   If I receive an email that I think should really have been a face-to-face conversation and if it's copied into others, I will try and answer the sender face to face and then visit the others to let them know I've dealt with it. I can't do this with everything of course, but it starts sending a signal. One of the leading pioneers in our digital world, Hewlett Packard originated the term 'leadership by wandering about' in the 70's and it's rather ironic that due to a lack of leadership focus, their digital systems have had the opposite effect.

5. Step back from your organization and take an honest look at how much people are really connecting with each other. 'I've emailed Fred time and time again, explaining how to do that' is very different from 'I showed Fred how to do that' or 'Fred and I spent some time together going through that and he seemed completely comfortable with it'. If you were; trying to get to the root cause of a problem or implement a new complex system or create a vital new product and you were asking your organization how things were going, imagine how much more confidence you would have in your teams if the responses were more like the last one than the first.

6. If your philosophy on work/life is to keep them separate and you're a fan of physical presenteeism, then consider disabling email servers outside of work hours. This might be difficult for organizations that operate on a 24hr basis and/or across time zones of course, but the principle should be considered. At the very least, employees (including senior managers) could be strongly advised not to email out of hours. Most email clients allow delayed sending so if you must write a note at midnight, set it to send no earlier than the start of the working day.

7. If your philosophy is more toward digital presenteeism, i.e. you'd rather your employees have a choice about when to respond to digital communications (or indeed any communications), then you might want to consider your approach generally to work/life balance. If you are going to give your employees this kind of choice, it might need to be mixed with an overall choice about when to work. I might want to spend a lazy Sunday catching up with emails in my garden, or writing that important report but to avoid overload, could reasonably expect some downtime elsewhere in the week.

8. It's probably worth saying that we shouldn't demonize email. In today's increasingly open-plan working environments, an employee

might prefer to have non-urgent question sent by email, rather than be distracted from a current flow state, addressing a complex problem.

Until Fred can hop into that holodeck and interrogate a computer for insights in the same way two people can problem solve together, Fred won't learn how to do it. Even with the holodeck, if you believe philosophically in the richness and unique creativity of human beings, Fred will only learn best and be most satisfied when he has learnt with another human being.

I think this is perhaps the most important consideration and deserves a few more soul-searching questions, because there is no soul in email. How much has technology connected your organization together and at the same time alienated your people? Is the superficiality of your internal communication increasing along with the volume of those communications? Are everyone 'busy fools', conducting the *illusion of work* and actually achieving very little? How much employee satisfaction and shareholder value is all of this creating, or destroying?

You need to investigate this, set a strategy to explore and find out what's really going on inside your organization. Brave leaders need to get out from behind their screens and challenge that firehose.

Key Learning Points for Leaders

If we accept that for now, technology alone won't provide the solution to IT's challenges, then the solution needs to come from our business leaders. This is a cultural challenge rather than a technological one and requires recognition and focus at tactical and strategic levels.

Connecting digital technologies can amplify irrational feelings of self-doubt and fear of missing out. A good chunk of our IT-derived work-based stress comes from an unhealthy adult-child relationship with technology that needs to become an adult-adult one.

There are some tactics workers use to lessen the feeling of being a slave to the machine. These include; turning off notifications, shutting down background applications, using the right tools for the right job and taking a digital break once in a while. Note we are not suggesting a return to a pre-digital age; we are not disconnectionist Luddites. As individuals, we need to recognize though when it's time to unplug.

We need employee-focused digital leadership strategies in the same way that we have marketing, IT and product strategies. When we procure new IT systems, we should ask suppliers to show how they consider digital overload both in system design and implementation. Digital overload should be on the agenda at senior meetings and be part of influencing organizational culture. HR Directors needs to take an honest look at how people are communicating (or not) and should adapt policies that deal with 'digital presenteeism'.

At the highest levels, you (whether a leader or a reader) need to ensure that the soul of your organization is not being diluted by the ubiquity of digital technology. To be frank; it's up to you.

12

Shifting Mindsets to Prepare for the Future

Susan Stucky and Jim Ware

While digital overload is experienced individually and personally, the sources of overload at work are not, for the most part, under individual control. The human experience of work is dramatically different in this digital age. Too, leadership has seemingly 'hit the wall' when it comes to directly addressing digital overload. We look ahead to a future where Artificial Intelligence threatens to take over the jobs performed by many professionals and ask how we might see the remaining work distributed.

S. Stucky (✉) · J. Ware
FutureWork Forum, California, USA
e-mail: susanstucky@gmail.com

J. Ware
e-mail: jim@thefutureofwork.net

© The Author(s) 2018
P. Thomson et al. (eds.), *Conquering Digital Overload*,
https://doi.org/10.1007/978-3-319-63799-0_12

Overview

We begin this chapter with a review of three kinds of experience with digital technology that ultimately lead to that sense of overload. These are such familiar experiences that people often respond with either annoyance or outright cynicism.

1. The almost universal ubiquity of digital technology. It's everywhere. It's with us all the time. This new reality contributes to a sense that it is beyond individuals' control. And, in many ways, it is, but that is not a reason for leaders and their organizations to avoid responsibility.
2. The all-too-common experience that digital technologies are not always helpful in getting work done. In particular, at the beginning, using new technology often feels as if it is creating 'make work.' It drives people to distraction. People create workarounds just to do what they are already used to doing.
3. Work that is getting done is becoming less and less visible. It is literally disappearing into the digital ether. Files seemingly disappear. 'Help me find it' is <u>still</u> a reason people call the help desk or reach out to friends. With the Cloud and the emergence of new, competing suites of 'office tools' such as Apple, Google, and IBM's offerings, we are seemingly back in the days of the multiple work processors that characterized the 80's.

These problems are unsolvable on their own; at least as they are presently defined. More and better interface design could help (but only if it reflects how people actually do their work). Automation is here to stay. Moreover, people are being told to expect to *collaborate* with technology to get their work done.

Their examination of these all-too-familiar sources of stress has prompted the authors to classify these challenges as perhaps more easily solved with new mindsets. As a starter for new ways of thinking, three mindset shifts are outlined in the last section of this chapter. The proof, as always, will be in the pudding.

But first we want to explore these three kinds of experience in more depth.

The Ubiquity of Digital Devices in the World of Work

The so-called 'digital age' is characterized by our deep, continuous and broad dependence on technology in virtually every aspect of our lives. Work is no exception. Increasingly the very same devices are used, often at the same time, for both work and in our everyday lives: a truly 'blended' existence. This 'intrusion' in both aspects of our experience intensifies that feeling of being overwhelmed and 'can't get away from it' that is fostered by the ubiquity of digital technology.

It is important to remember that digital technology in all its forms enables people to connect, in real time, in video, with almost anyone else in the world at very low incremental cost. Additionally, anyone with an Internet connection or mobile phone access can use a search engine to access almost any information no matter where in the world it is located; and anyone can publish any kind of information globally (through websites, blogs, and social media), again at very little incremental cost. It is the same basic technology whether we use it at work or in our everyday lives.

It's everywhere and there is a whole lot of it. Gartner Group estimates that in 2015 there were about 5 billion devices connected to the Internet. The number of 'conversations' among those devices far exceeds the number of conversations among human beings: everything from temperature sensors to motion detectors to listening/recording devices, video cameras, mobile phones, ATM's, automobiles, oil refineries, key chain holders, and fast-food drive-in order stations.[97] Sensors measure weather patterns, moisture in the ground, and highway traffic; artificial intelligence drives capabilities like Apple's Siri and Amazon's Echo. Automated processes calculate airplane weight loads and fuel requirements based on passenger check-in data. They also charge credit card accounts without any human intervention (based on pre-defined algorithms and personal permission), execute stock trades, adjust thermostats, and count pedestrian traffic.

Increasingly we hear talk of 'smart buildings,' 'smart cities,' 'smart refrigerators,' 'smart homes,' 'smart cars,' and even smart dolls. Automated factories can operate in 'lights out' mode to produce complex products at much lower cost, and higher quality, than more traditional industrial factories ever could.

We hardly need to make the case that work and life today are deeply dependent on technology. And the net result is that, for many of us, life and work is in general much richer and far more enjoyable than ever.

The digital age seems to have exploded on society without thoughtful planning or any warning, and that simple reality is itself a cause of stress and anxiety. Even more significant is the all-too-common experience of having to learn new ways of getting things done. For example, learning how to speak to Siri so she/he can respond with meaningful information (directions, addresses, telephone numbers, your friend's birthday).

As author Kevin Kelly has pointed out, one of the most basic attributes of modern digital technology is that every digital device and each software application is 'buggy' (less than perfect) and is continually being upgraded and ostensibly, improved at a much more rapid pace than many people are able to deal with.[98]

That means that we are all permanent 'newbies' (Kelly's term). We must invest precious time learning how each new version of these tools we depend on works, to say nothing of the time we lose while the technology is undergoing the latest upgrade, and then all the adjusting we must do to the settings, options, storage choices, and more of our favorite applications.

We are continually being inundated by new products, all purporting to be 'faster, cheaper, better' than the existing tools we've finally just become familiar with.

Add to that the fact that often those new products were invented to solve problems we didn't know we had, so our beliefs about what is possible are constantly being challenged.

For example, before Steve Jobs introduced the iPod, did you know you wanted 'a thousand songs in your pocket'? That was the way he described the iPod when he held up the first one at the product announcement event. The iPod is a perfect example of a product that created its own demand, though it now faces competition from streaming. The other prime example for older fossils, like us, is the Polaroid instant camera, that created its own market from nothing decades ago.

It is common in Silicon Valley to depend on engineers and technicians for new product ideas, and to dismiss market research as irrelevant. After all, you can't expect consumers to provide useful data about a product they have never seen that solves a 'problem' they are oblivious to.

At the same time, designers and software architects/engineers are coming to realize that they can't predict all the effects of the software they design and develop. Once it leaves their hands and is integrated with other systems, there is literally no way to anticipate everything that can happen going forward.

Then, of course, there is the stress that comes from owning a laptop or mobile phone that is several years old, and knowing that you are behind the times because you don't have the latest and greatest. If being 'with it' is important, you find yourself investing frequently in new, upgraded versions of technology devices even though the ones you have meet your basic needs just fine, thank you very much.

The ubiquity of digital devices isn't good or bad in itself. In fact, digital technologies aren't good or bad in themselves altogether, so thinking of them as inherently good or bad isn't going to help with the overwhelm factor.

Digital Technologies are not Always Helpful

Of course, the primary reason that so many business processes have been fully or partially automated is that technology can make those processes less expensive, faster, more reliable, and easier to deploy. However, none of those results is guaranteed. All too often an automated or augmented process doesn't make sense to a human actor who needs to use the technology or benefit from the process's completion. It's confusing. How and why it works the way it works remains opaque to the user.

One reason for this discomfort is that there is too little understanding about how work is actually getting done. This often comes about because the designers' methods for defining 'requirements' don't reveal how the work is actually done.

Susan Stucky has many years' experience in fielding teams and being part of teams that analyze how work actually gets done for design, whether for facilities, technology, business process, organizations, or all four. She notes that there are often more people involved in getting the work done than are acknowledged; in one case by a factor of four!

The people doing the work on a daily basis often also use technologies and tools in places that aren't evident in a cursory study. Also, the more the work sediments out into work practice: (the way people do work together) the less visible it becomes to the people doing it.

Getting work done in organizational contexts usually includes at least some steps that are so complex and situationally variable that they cannot be reduced to stable algorithms that can be coded into software. That is, completing the process to produce the 'right' result still depends on human problem-solving that is not amenable to automation. Without understanding the work practice, it is not even known where the journey, the transformation, has to start.

In some cases, management wants a system to be designed in a particular way in order to achieve the promised business benefit. Mistakenly they think that just because they don't want people to be doing the work the way they were before, how they get it done now isn't relevant to the future. There are many stakeholders at hand in the design and development of new technologies and they have, often, competing agendas.

In one case, Susan was involved with a case that not only generated work-arounds, but led to outright rebellion. Management had wanted costing and pricing of a service offering to be standardized for the company. It was thought that eliminating the use of spreadsheets on the part of humans could aid in controlling that process.

The problem was that the pricers and costers had to work with customers who wanted 'what ifs'. What if we do this instead of that? But without the use of spreadsheets developed by the users over years and years, the pricers and costers were hamstrung. One spreadsheet virtuoso had 57 spreadsheets open at once!

In the end, workbooks were reintroduced. The work practice, the way costers did their work, was not understood to begin with. In fact, the developers and management didn't feel the need to understand it because they wanted people to work in a new way, without recourse to non-standard pricing and costing. In a sense, they really did not *want* to understand the old way. After all, technology applications are, for the most part, designed by human beings (though that too is changing), and people inevitably embed their often-imperfect understanding of how a process operates within the systems they create.

Unhelpful digital technology also arises because there has been a growing belief among system designers that 'getting it done today beats getting it perfect.' That is, it's more valuable to get an incomplete, buggy system into production and then rely on end users to discover and report its deficiencies, than to spend many more days or months trying to get it perfect before sharing it with the world.

For example, Facebook has long bragged about having a 24-hour 'go-live' update cycle for its base operating platform. New ideas, as well as corrected algorithms, are included in these daily system 'upgrades' even though the 'improvement' often seemingly exists only in the minds of the system designers. In fact, many of those changes, especially with respect to permissions and privacy, make Facebook more challenging for the millions of people who interact with the system every day.

In fact, this mode of operation, often called agile development, is reflective of another interaction among digital systems, producing outcomes that weren't anticipated, and arguably *cannot* be anticipated, as we will see below.

All too often digital systems are designed to appeal to everyone, and thus they end up pleasing no one. Take, for example, the Microsoft Office suite (Word, Excel, PowerPoint, Outlook, Project, and several less widely used applications). Those basic office tools have become so bloated with features and options that it can take months or years to learn what is possible.

Who hasn't had the experience of suddenly discovering a feature in Word that you didn't know was there, even though you had been using the product for years? The net result of trying to offer something for everyone from the casual typist or letter writer to the most sophisticated copy editor, book author, technical writer, or daily blogger is that the product features are overwhelming for almost everyone. As the late futurist, Alvin Toffler once remarked, 'One size misfits all.'[99]

Digital technologies become more and more unhelpful as they are designed to address more and more complexity, especially that which wasn't anticipated. Only a very few technologists foresaw the extent and aggressiveness of hacking, for instance. Privacy and security are essential but at the same time introduce even more things to do and worry about while working.

Interaction Between and Among Digital Technologies Compounds the Problem of Invisible Work

What happens as more and more systems 'talk' with each other, with no human involvement, as they are combined and recombined, and as software programs are refactored, optimized, and fall by the wayside?

Think about how hard it would be to understand the digital underpinnings of customer experience. It is now impossible to figure out how the customer experience of a trip is assured, because of the entanglement of digital systems. Business processes are automated and then the software programs are further combined, their code optimized again and again.

It is actually much worse than files disappearing, as annoying as that is. As the economist Brian Arthur pointed out in a McKinsey article in 2011, it is as if there is a second economy, a digital one running in parallel with the physical one we know.

> If I were to look for adjectives to describe this second economy, I'd say it is vast, silent, connected, unseen, and autonomous (meaning that human beings may design it but are not directly involved in running it). It is remotely executing and global, always on, and endlessly configurable. It is concurrent, a great computer expression, which means that everything happens in parallel. It is self-configuring, meaning it constantly reconfigures itself on the fly, and increasingly it is also self-organizing, self-architecting, and self-healing.[100]

Why does Arthur describe the digital world of work as an economy? Susan once asked Brian, who gave the answer that is in his book, The Nature of Technology, as 'the set of arrangements and actions we use to meet our needs in society.'[101]

Arthur's best example of the invisible digital economy at work is that of checking in for a flight. Whether on-line via desktop or mobile or at an airport kiosk, the whole thing looks like a grand conversation. Arthur says it so well that a full quote is included here.

> ...you are starting a huge conversation conducted entirely among machines. Once your name is recognized, computers are checking your flight status with the airlines, your past travel history, your name with the TSA (airport security) and possibly also with the National Security Agency. They are checking your seat choice, your frequent-flier status, and your access to lounges. This unseen, underground conversation is happening among multiple servers talking to other servers, talking to satellites that are talking to computers (possibly in London, where you're going), and checking with passport control, with foreign immigration, with ongoing connecting flights. And to make sure the aircraft's weight distribution is fine, the machines are also starting to adjust the passenger count and seating according to whether the fuselage is loaded more heavily at the front or back.
>
> These large and fairly complicated conversations that you've triggered occur entirely among things remotely talking to other things: servers, switches, routers, and other Internet and telecommunications devices, updating and shuttling information back and forth. All of this occurs in the few seconds it takes to get your boarding pass back. And even after that happens, if you could see these conversations as flashing lights, they'd still be flashing all over the country for some time, perhaps talking to the flight controllers, starting to say that the flight's getting ready for departure and to prepare for that.

Upon reflection, Arthur's definition seems just right. '*A set of digital arrangements and actions that is being used to meet our needs as a society*' is exactly what that digital world needs to be. As already pointed out, knowledge work, the doing of knowledge work, has always been hard to see even when people are doing it. Thinking is hard to see. A conversation may not look like knowledge work is being done, even though that is a primary way people co-create knowledge. The output of knowledge work is only part of the picture. Rather, the outcome, the impact of the work, may be a long time coming. The same is now true of the digital work that technology is doing.

New Ways of Working and New Ways of Thinking

This list of complaints around working digitally could go on and on. And in a sense, one way to address this state-of-affairs is to recognize it for what it is: a societal and cultural problem that is hard to solve, or even unsolvable. Even when broken down into smaller problems, the smaller problems seem unsolvable or in the end, don't generate a satisfactory outcome, or worse, have unintended consequences.

There is a suggestion we can take from the people who have coined and wrested with what they call 'wicked problems'[102] Here what is suggested is not solutions to problems, so much as a *resolution*.

A resolution requires a shift in mindset, perhaps several shifts by several different groups of people. Changing mindsets, such as going from the belief that the world is flat to its being round, is an example. That shift has enabled accomplishments that would have been impossible otherwise. Going to the moon, for instance would have been difficult to accomplish under the flat world mindset.

Brian Arthur's observation that there is a digital economy humming along, largely invisible, unseen, and inscrutable certainly could be viewed as a wicked problem; if the digital economy is not altogether out of control, it is certainly out of *our* control.

But resolution doesn't show up in its full glory all at once. It emerges after people, doing what they do, run up against roadblocks and change their mindsets. We suggest the following three mindset shifts, each relevant to digital overload in the face of a second, digital economy as a way to move forward. In this case they are suggested by how we can understand knowledge work for people and technologies as discussed in Chap. 6.

Mindset Shift Number 1: Design for Outcome

Recently, the American Association of Computing Machinery (ACM) in a Tech News email[n] [103]pointed to a new algorithm developed by researchers at the Nanyang Technological University (NTU) in

Singapore. It is designed to reduce the number of 'spontaneous traffic jams across a roadway network.' What is new is not that there is yet another traffic calming algorithm, but how the researchers thought about it.

Technically, their design insight was to achieve their goal, to maximize the probability that none of the network links [road intersections] encounters a breakdown, with the AI technique of machine learning. The machine 'learns' from numbers of real-life examples, and the algorithm is modified, getting better and better. If the roads change, the algorithm can change right along with it. It was resolved by thinking about it differently, as re-directing traffic, not just re-designing the road system.

This example demonstrates several important points. First, the researchers are working toward an outcome, not an output, which is the same kind of measure that we pointed out in the chapter on knowledge work.

Indeed, the technology can be seen to be doing (digital) work that looks a whole lot like knowledge work. Second, roadways, like digital technologies, are designed to reward the behavior of individual human actors, but have the unintended consequence of getting in the way of moving many cars. The solution isn't to design to reward the behavior of the individuals in a different way, say by staggering commute times, or limiting the number of cars, but by designing to a different outcome.

As a colleague has expressed to one of us, he doesn't want or not want an autonomous car. He does want people to be able to be more independent; for his parents to be able to stay in their house longer. That is an outcome, not an output.

Mindset Shift Number 2: Design not just for Human-Computer Interaction, but a New Kind of Human-Computer 'Conversation'

As pointed out in the chapter about knowledge work (Chap. 6), there has been an either/or stance to the relationship between digital technology and the work humans do: whether to *automate* or to *augment* human activity and capabilities. One might think, both work, so why not figure out which works better in what kind of situation?

For instance, should driving be automated? Or should it continue on the trajectory of providing assistance, as in the case of car parking, or augmenting medical diagnosis? Frankly, it is hard to imagine resolving this in organizational settings, never mind in society as a whole.

We believe there is another way to think about it. Here is another lesson from knowledge-based work, a parallel. Conversations are one way that people co-create knowledge. (Okay, there is another mindset shift needed here: people don't learn knowledge; knowledge is co-created by people, and, now, by people and machines working together). But as Brian Arthur noted, digital technologies hold ongoing conversations triggered by a human doing a simple thing like checking in at an airport kiosk or, now, checking in on their mobile phone. The endless conversations that digital technologies have with each other, as in Arthur's observation, are largely unseen, although, goodness knows, it is not as if people need or want to see all of them.

What about designing digital technology not just for human-computer interaction, but for human-computer conversation? A medical diagnosis with IBM's Watson-based physician's assistant looks a whole lot like that, but it took at a number of years for that mindset shift to take place at IBM. People learn from each other. Arguably people can learn from machines. What if humans and machines can have interactions that are more like conversations (and yes, there is a whole field of conversation analysis)?[104]

Mindset Shift Number 3: Focus on Managing Work; Foster Work-Centric Thinking

Presently there is a certain urgency to the admonition to focus on work triggered, in part, by the explosion of options in how to get work done. Hence, this section goes into more detail on the mindset shift. The rise of freelancing, crowdsourcing, contests, and contractors, along with many other forms of contingent workers, presents a wide array of choice in who is eligible to do the work. It also presents choice about where it can be done, when it gets done, and what payment mechanism should be used. As a result of this new variety of work practices, the cost to get the work done and the price a person doing the work is willing to settle for is now dependent on the particular array of choices to be made, not the cost of labor.

When she was serving in the research function at a large IT company, a project arrived on Susan's doorstep. The HR function was in the middle of imagining a very-long term future for HR. The HR staff came up with the idea of a 'Talent Cloud.' The expectation was of a fairly straightforward 'design and build' technology development that would match talent, or skills, to project needs.

This approach has been tried in many companies and with many technologies, and falls short for a straightforward reason: parsing people into skills, and projects into sets of skills presumes that the people who need to get the work done will know what skills are needed. But in today's fragmenting world, that is increasingly hard, if not impossible, to do.

The Death of Work?

Predictions that digital technology will replace human labor have been around for decades. So far we have seen shifts in skill sets needed to do work, but no major unemployment as a result. We no longer need telephone switchboard operators or punch card input workers. But we have created work for website designers and games developers instead. Computers have replaced some routine human tasks but not yet made serious inroads to replacing human judgment and creativity.

The Internet has spawned websites and applications that have also replaced human jobs. Customers now buy their insurance through comparison sites and book hotels and flights without needing a travel agent. Yet, unemployment hasn't soared as a result. We now have economies that have produced work for people who provide a variety of services, from walking dogs to caring for an ageing population. So new jobs have emerged to replace old ones that are no longer needed.

Information is readily available over the Internet and with the aid of search engines can be located without expert advice. When all the legal cases in the world are available on your personal computer, why do you need a lawyer? When Wikipedia can give you an answer to most questions you might want to ask, why do you need to speak to an expert? The answer to this is simple. What you need is knowledge, what you get is information. So you still need the professional to give expert advice. You might be able to look up your medical symptoms on the Web, but you still need a doctor to add expert knowledge and understanding to give a diagnosis. Human judgment is still needed to interpret the data.

But now the world is changing. Artificial Intelligence (AI) is able to make those decisions that until now have been reserved for humans. Computers can now learn how to solve problems and not follow instructions. They can replace professional advisors and give a better quality of advice. In their well researched book,[106] father and son team, Richard and Daniel Suskind look in depth at the future of the professions. They challenge the view that there are many tasks that are not susceptible to computerization because they are 'non-routine'. It is a fallacy to suppose the only way to develop systems that perform non-routine tasks is to replicate the thinking processes of human specialists. They say 'machines can perform very demanding tasks, and often outperform human beings by operating in entirely different ways from human beings. Increasingly capable machines, we conclude, will gradually take on more non-routine tasks; and so the intuition that there will always be tasks left that only humans can perform will prove to be ill-founded'

This raises the fundamental question. Will there be enough work to go around in the future? And if we have replaced humans with technology what will we do with the time available? If we no longer need drivers for cars, taxis, buses and trains where will those people go? If doctors, lawyers, teachers and journalists can be replaced by AI, will we have a middle class unemployment problem?

Then the critical question is 'How will the work be distributed?'. Will we finally have the life of leisure promised by the technological revolution and only need to work two or three days a week? Or will there be 'Haves' and 'Have-nots' with some people still working long hours and others with no paid work? Will human ingenuity, as it has, rise to the challenge?

So far, technology has not brought the life of leisure. This book argues that it has had the reverse effect. We have more stress and longer working hours than ever before. But maybe that's just a phase between the 3rd and 4th Industrial Revolutions. We have added digital technology to an analogue world and not adjusted our work patterns in line with it. The developments in technology have outstripped our ability to adjust. As the true digital natives take over the world of work, perhaps it will catch up. But will this happen with a smooth evolution led by inspired leaders, or will it be a revolution with out-of-touch leaders being toppled by a combination of market pressure and employee dissatisfaction? We hope it will be the former, but without leaders recognizing and addressing the issues we have raised in this book and applying some of the suggested solutions, we fear it will be the latter.

Key Learnings for Leaders

Work is becoming less visible and less comprehensible as computers exchange information and run algorithms without human intervention.

Digital Overload is a societal and cultural problem that is hard to solve. The resolution comes from shifts in mindset from leaders.

Shift 1. Manage outcomes not just outputs.

Shift 2. Design work for humans to have 'conversations' with computers not just with each other

Shift 3. Focus on managing work not just on tasks and skills.

We are on the brink of an AI revolution which will potentially replace many knowledge work jobs. Leaders have a window of opportunity to redesign work and reduce Digital Overload as we introduce new technologies.

Notes

1. World Economic Forum, 2015, Are you ready for the technological revolution? https://www.weforum.org/agenda/2015/02/are-you-ready-for-the-technological-revolution.
2. MIT, 2012, The Digital Advantage: How digital leaders outperform their peers in every industry.
3. Jeff DesJardins, April 25 2016, What happens in an Internet minute?, Excelacom, http://www.visualcapitalist.com/what-happens-internet-minute-2016/. Accessed 7 June 2017.
4. 3 Gallup, 2013, State of the American Workplace.
5. EURACTIV Germany, 2015 https://www.euractiv.com/section/health-consumers/news/german-economy-burdened-by-growing-rate-of-depression/. Accessed 6 June 2017.
6. European Agency for Safety and Health at Work, 2014, Calculating the costs of work-related stress and psychosocial risks.
7. Robert Half, 2013, https://www.roberthalf.co.uk/press/employee-burnout-common-nearly-third-uk-companies-say-hr-directors. Accessed 8 June 2017.

© The Editor(s) (if applicable) and The Author(s) 2018
P. Thomson et al. (eds.), *Conquering Digital Overload*,
https://doi.org/10.1007/978-3-319-63799-0

8. International Labour Organization, 2016, Workplace Stress, http://www.ilo.org/wcmsp5/groups/public/—ed_protect/—protrav/—safework/documents/publication/wcms_466547.pdf   Accessed   8 June 2017.

9. Hilbert M (2012) How much information is there in the 'information society'? University of Southern California.

10. Ernst and Young, (2016) 'The gig economy: transforming the workforce'. (PDF)

11. Radicati Group (2016) Email Statistics Report. http://www.radicati.com/wp/wp-content/uploads/2016/01/Email_Statistics_Report_2016-2020_Executive_Summary.pdf. Accessed 6 June 2017.

12. Mckinsey Global Institute (2012) The Social Economy: Unlocking value and productivity through social technology. http://www.mckinsey.com/industries/high-tech/our-insights/the-social-economy. Accessed 6 June 2017.

13. CIPD (2017) Employee Outlook, Spring 2017. https://www.cipd.co.uk/Images/employee-outlook_2017-spring_tcm18-21163.pdf. Accessed 6 June 2017.

14. Ibid.

15. Bennett R. (2016) Ignore that cc and delete that inbox. The Times https://www.thetimes.co.uk/article/a60233b4-31ab-11e6-9c43-b579056ef2e5. Accessed 15 Feb 2017.

16. World Health Organisation, (2017) Depression: Let's talk. http://www.who.int/mediacentre/news/releases/2017/world-health-day/en/. Accessed 14 May 2017.

17. Bersin J. (2016) Predictions for 2017. Bersin by Deloitte. https://www2.deloitte.com/content/dam/Deloitte/at/Documents/about-deloitte/predictions-for-2017-final.pdf. Accessed 6 June 2017.

18. Matrix, (on behalf of the EU) (2013) Economic analysis of workplace mental health promotion and mental disorder prevention programmes and of their potential contribution to EU health, social and economic policy objectives. http://ec.europa.eu/health//sites/health/files/mental_health/docs/matrix_economic_analysis_mh_promotion_en.pdf. Accessed 6 June 2017.

19. Newbery C. (2015) Annual cost of presenteeism is 'twice that of absenteeism', says Prof Cary Cooper. People Management. http://www2.cipd.co.uk/pm/peoplemanagement/b/weblog/archive/2015/11/04/annual-cost-of-presenteeism-is-twice-that-of-absenteeism-says-prof-cooper.aspx. Accessed 1 Feb 2017.

20. American Psychological Association, (2015) Stress in America: paying with our health. https://www.apa.org/news/press/releases/stress/2014/stress-report.pdf. Accessed 6 June 2017.

21. Perlow L.A., Porter J.L. (2009) Making time off predictable – and required. Harvard Business Review https://hbr.org/2009/10/making-time-off-predictable-and-required. Accessed 15 Feb 2017.

22. Heskett, J., Sasser, W., Schlesinger, L., (1997) The Service Profit Chain. The Free Press, New York.

23. Gallup (2016) Meta Q12®; The Relationship Between Engagement at Work and Organizational Outcomes http://www.gallup.com/services/191489/q12-meta-analysis-report-2016.aspx. Accessed 6 June 2017.

24. Bersin J. (2016) Predictions for 2017. Bersin by Deloitte. https://www2.deloitte.com/content/dam/Deloitte/at/Documents/about-deloitte/predictions-for-2017-final.pdf. Accessed 6 June 2017.

25. Porath C. (2016) The hidden toll of workplace incivility. McKinsey Quarterly http://www.mckinsey.com/business-functions/organization/our-insights/the-hidden-toll-of-workplace-incivility?cid=other-alt-mkq-mck-oth-1612. Accessed 10 March 2017.

26. Ernst and Young, (2016) The gig economy: transforming the workplace.

27. Harvard Business Review, (2012) The rise of the new contract worker. https://hbr.org/2012/09/the-rise-of-the-new-contract-worker. Accessed 12 Jan 2017.

28. New York Times, (2013) A focus on distraction. http://www.nytimes.com/2013/05/05/opinion/sunday/a-focus-on-distraction.html. Accessed 15 Jan 2017.

29. Stanford University, (2009) Media multi-taskers pay mental price. http://news.stanford.edu/2009/08/24/multitask-research-study-082409/. Accessed 12 Jan 2017.

30. Forbes, (2014) Multi-tasking damages your health and career. https://www.forbes.com/sites/travisbradberry/2014/10/08/multitasking-damages-your-brain-and-career-new-studies-suggest/#3725b76d56ee. Accessed 12 Jan 2017.
31. Eurekalert, (2014) Brain scans reveal 'gray matter' differences in media multitaskers https://www.eurekalert.org/pub_releases/2014-09/uos-bsr092314.php. Accessed 12 Jan 2017.
32. Realization, (2013) The effect of multitasking on organizations. http://www.realization.com/pdf/Effects_of_Multitasking_on_Organizations.pdf. Accessed 15 Jan 2017.
33. Barabel M., Meier O. (2015) Le Management à l'Ere Digitale. Manageor Dunod.
34. OECD (2016) Automation and Independent Work in a Digital Economy. http://www.oecd.org/employment/Policy%20brief%20-%20Automation%20and%20Independent%20Work%20in%20a%20Digital%20Economy.pdf. Accessed 6 June 2017.
35. Jensen J. (2017) Mangers and Technostress. Presentation to Henley Forum Conference. March 2nd 2017.
36. David Drennan, (1992) Transforming Company Culture, McGraw Hill.
37. CIPD Employee Outlook Spring 2017 (2017) https://www.cipd.co.uk/knowledge/fundamentals/relations/engagement/employee-outlook-reports. Accessed 6 June 2017.
38. Lewis G. (2015) Long Hours Culture rising again after decades of decline, analysis reveals. People Management, 10 September 2015 http://www2.cipd.co.uk/pm/peoplemanagement/b/weblog/archive/2015/09/10/long-hours-culture-rising-again-after-decades-of-decline-analysis-reveals.aspx. Accessed 4 June 2017.
39. CIPD Employee Outlook Spring 2017 (2017) https://www.cipd.co.uk/knowledge/fundamentals/relations/engagement/employee-outlook-reports. Accessed 6 June 2017.
40. Capgemini Consulting (2017) The Digital Culture Challenge: Closing the Employee-Leadership Gap. https://www.capgemini-consulting.com/resource-file-access/resource/pdf/dti_digitalculture_report.pdf Accessed 9 June 2017.

41. BBC News, 22 March 2002. Mobiles 'worse than drink-driving' http://news.bbc.co.uk/1/hi/uk/1885775.stm. Accessed 4 June 2017.

42. Feser C., Mayol F., Srinivasan R. (2015) Decoding Leadership: What really matters. McKinsey Quarterly January 2015. www.mckinsey.com/global-themes/leadership/decoding-leadership-what-really-matters. Accessed 4 June 2017.

43. Forrester Consulting (2014) The Creative Dividend: How creativity impacts business results. http://landing.adobe.com/dam/downloads/whitepapers/55563.en.creative-dividends.pdf. Accessed 4 June 2017.

44. Trafton A. (2014) In the blink of an eye. MIT News, 16 January 2014. http://news.mit.edu/2014/in-the-blink-of-an-eye-0116. Accessed 6 June 2017.

45. Robinson K. (2005) Do schools kill creativity? TED talk, February 2005 https://www.ted.com/talks/ken_robinson_says_schools_kill_creativity. Accessed 4 June 2017.

46. Frayne D. (2015). *The Refusal of Work: The Theory and Practice of Resistance to Work.* Zed Books, London.

47. Norden A. (2017) Putting IBM Watson to the Test For Cancer Care. Forbes, January 26, 2017 https://www.forbes.com/sites/ibm/2017/01/26/putting-ibm-watson-to-the-test-for-cancer-care/#53fc5db24990. Accessed 26 April 2017.

48. Nye D.E. (2013) America's Assembly Line. MIT Press, Cambridge, MA: MIT Press (p. 252).

49. Malone T.W. (2004) The Future of Work. MIT Press, Cambridge, Mass.

50. Engelbart, D.C. (1995). 'Toward augmenting the human intellect and boosting our collective IQ' (PDF). Communications of the ACM. 38 (8): 30. doi:10.1145/208344.208352.

51. Drucker P.F. (1959) The Landmarks of Tomorrow. Harper and Row, New York.

52. Ware J.P. (2016) Making Meetings Matter. Indie Books International. Chapter 5, Finding the Place Just Right.

53. Riederle P. (2013) Presentation at 2013 annual conference of the National Speakers Association in Philadelphia.

54. Webber A. (1993) What's So New About the New Economy? Harvard Business Review, reprint #93109, January-February 1993.
55. Ware J.P. (2011) Flexible Work: Rhetoric and Reality. a Citrix Online White Paper. https://thefutureofwork.net/assets/Flexible_Work_Rhetoric_and_Reality.pdf. Accessed 25 April 2017.
56. Arthur W.B. (2011) The Second Economy. McKinsey Quarterly, October 2011.
57. See Chap. 11 for an extended discussion of this phenomenon.
58. Edgar Schein (2004) Organizational Culture and Leadership. Wiley, Page 2.
59. Ben Emmens (2016) Conscious Collaboration: Re-Thinking The Way We Work Together, For Good. Palgrave Macmillan.
60. The State of American Vacation (2017) Project time Off http://www.projecttimeoff.com/sites/default/files/StateofAmericanVacation2017.pdf.
61. Global Human Capital Trends 2014, Deloitte, https://dupress.deloitte.com/dup-us-en/focus/human-capital-trends/2014.htm. Accessed 4 June 2017.
62. Employee Outlook (2015) CIPD https://www.cipd.co.uk/Images/employee-outlook_2015_tcm18-10904.pdf. Accessed 4 June 2017.
63. Crabtree S. (2013) Gallup, October 8th 2013, http://www.gallup.com/poll/165269/worldwide-employees-engaged-work.aspx. Accessed 4 June 2017.
64. Pew Research Centre (2015) May 11th 2015 http://www.pewresearch.org/fact-tank/2015/05/11/millennials-surpass-gen-xers-as-the-largest-generation-in-u-s-labor-force/. Accessed 4 May 2017.
65. Bersin by Deloitte (2017) Predictions for 2017. https://www2.deloitte.com/content/dam/Deloitte/at/Documents/about-deloitte/predictions-for-2017-final.pdf. Accessed 4 June 2017.
66. Wolff K. (2014) Die besten Arbeitgeber der Start-up- und Digitalwelt. https://www.deutsche-startups.de/2014/12/09/die-besten-arbeitgeber-der-start-und-digitalwelt/. Accessed 4 June 2017.
67. Gründerszene (2017) Eine deutsche Startup-Erfolgsgeschichte auf 5 Etagen. http://www.gruenderszene.de/galerie/jimdo-buero?pid=11645. Accessed 4 June 2017.

68. Jimdo (2017) The top reasons you'll love working at Jimdo. https://www.jimdo.com/about-jimdo/working-at-jimdo/. Accessed 4 June 2017.
69. Freitag (2017) The Freitag Story. https://www.freitag.ch/en/about. Accessed 6 June 2017.
70. Heiko Fischer: www.resourceful-humans.com. Accessed 4 June 2017.
71. http://www.beyond-leadership.de/en/. Accessed 4 June 2017.
72. Cowden P.D. (2013) Neustart. Ariston.
73. Semler R. (2015) Radical wisdom for a company, a school, a life. https://www.youtube.com/watch?v=k4vzhweOefs. Accessed 4 June 2017.
74. Laloux F. (2014) Reinventing Organizations. Nelson Parker.
75. Clinard D. (2017) What do graduates look for in an employer? http://universumglobal.com/articles/2017/05/graduates-look-employer/. Accessed 4 June 2017.
76. Happiness Reigns: Meet Laurence Vanhée. http://www.ahead.be/news-a-views-from-ahead/headway-spring-2013/122-happiness-reigns-meet-laurence-vanhee.
77. International Facility Management Association, Space and Project Management Benchmarks, Research Report 34.
78. Scand J. (2011) Sickness absence associated with shared and open-plan offices–a national cross sectional questionnaire survey. Work Environ Health. 2011 Sep; 37(5):376–82. doi: 10.5271/sjweh.3167. Epub 2011 April 28.
79. Entis L. (2016) The Open-Office Concept is Dead. Fortune, May 12 2016 http://fortune.com/2016/05/12/the-open-office-concept-is-dead/. Accessed 6 June 2017.
80. Biggart L. (2015) Emotional Intelligence (EI) and performance in child and family social work. University of East Anglia https://www.uea.ac.uk/centre-research-child-family/child-protection-and-family-support/current-projects/emotional-intelligence-ei-and-performance-in-child-and-family-social-work. Accessed 6 June 2017.
81. CIPD Policy Report (2016) Growing the health and well-being agenda: From first steps to full potential.

82. PriceWaterhouseCoopers (2008) Building the case for wellness [online]. London: PricewaterhouseCoopers. https://www.gov.uk/government/uploads/system/uploads/attachment_data/file/209547/hwwb-dwp-wellness-report-public.pdf. Accessed 3 May 2017.

83. International Labour Organization, (2016) Workplace Stress: A collective Challenge http://www.ilo.org/wcmsp5/groups/public/—ed_protect/—protrav/—safework/documents/publication/wcms_466547.pdf. Accessed 3 May 2017.

84. Investors in People (2017) The Health and Wellbeing Award: An Overview. https://www.investorsinpeople.com/sites/default/files/2017_CIC_HWB_Web_0.pdf. Accessed 3 May 2017.

85. The Radicati Group Inc, (2015) Email Statistics Report, 2015-2019. http://www.radicati.com/wp/wp-content/uploads/2015/02/Email-Statistics-Report-2015-2019-Executive-Summary.pdf. Accessed 6 June 2017.

86. Dettmers J., Vahle-Hinz T., Bamberg E., et al. (2015) Extended Work Availability and Its Relation With Start-of-Day Mood and Cortisol. Journal of Occupational Health Psychology. Published online August 3 2015.

87. Morris D.Z, (2017) New French Law Bars Work Email After Hours. Fortunehttp://fortune.com/2017/01/01/french-right-to-disconnect-law. Accessed 6 June 2017.

88. Bennett A. (2014) British Bosses Should Follow German Ministry's Idea To Stop Burnout, Say Experts. Huffington Post UK. http://www.huffingtonpost.co.uk/2014/04/02/germany-staff-stress-burnout_n_5075150.html. Accessed 6 June 2017.

89. Ibid.

90. Pink D. (2010) Drive: The surprising truth about what motivates us. RSA Animate. YouTube. https://www.youtube.com/watch?v=u6XAPnuFjJc. Accessed 6 June 2017.

91. Kellaway L. (2015) A blast of common sense frees staff from appraisals. Financial Times July 26th 2015 https://www.ft.com/content/8e3ae550-3166-11e5-8873-775ba7c2ea3d. Accessed 6 June 2017.

92. Kasparov G (2017) Don't fear intelligent machine. Work With them. TED Talk April 2017 https://www.ted.com/talks/garry_kasparov_don_t_fear_intelligent_machines_work_with_them. Accessed 6 June 2017.

93. Gallo A. (2012) Stop email overload. Harvard Business Review, February 21st 2012 https://hbr.org/2012/02/stop-email-overload-1. Accessed 6 June 2017.

94. Ibid.

95. BBC News (2012) Atos boss Thierry Breton defends his internal email ban. BBC News Website, 8 March 2012. http://www.bbc.co.uk/news/technology-16055310. Accessed 6 June 2017.

96. Burkus D. (2016) Why Atos Origin Is Striving To Be A Zero-Email Company, Forbes Online, July 12th 2016, https://www.forbes.com/sites/davidburkus/2016/07/12/why-atos-origin-is-striving-to-be-a-zero-email-company/#f6ba1ea8d0ff. Accessed 6 June 2017.

97. Gartner (2014) Gartner Says 4.9 Billion Connected "Things" Will Be in Use in 2015 http://www.gartner.com/newsroom/id/2905717. Accessed 17 February 2017.

98. Kelly K. (2016) The Inevitable: Understanding the 12 Technological Forces that will Shape our Future. Viking, New York.

99. Toffler A. private conversation with Jim Ware.

100. Arthur W.B. (2011) The Second Economy. *McKinsey Quarterly*, October 2011.

101. Arthur, W.B. (2009) The Nature of Technology: What it is and How it Evolves. Free Press, New York, p. 192.

102. Churchman C.W. (1967) Wicked Problems. *Management Science*. 14 (4). doi:10.1287/mnsc.14.4.B141.

103. ACM Technews (2017) New AI Algorithm Beats Even the World's Worst Traffic. https://cacm.acm.org/news/215167-new-ai-algorithm-beats-even-the-worlds-worst-traffic/fulltext. Accessed 27 March 2017.

104.   Wikipedia (2017) Conversation Analysis https://en.wikipedia. org/wiki/Conversation_analysis. Accessed 09 May 2017.

105.   Stucky S.U. (2013) Work Marketplaces: Whither the Workplace. in Workplace Strategy Summit: Research in Action, published by the IFMA Foundation.

106.   Suskind R., and Suskind D. (2015) The Future of the Professions. Oxford University Press P. 294.

Index

© The Editor(s) (if applicable) and The Author(s) 2018
P. Thomson et al. (eds.), *Conquering Digital Overload*,
https://doi.org/10.1007/978-3-319-63799-0

Printed by Printforce, the Netherlands